THE WORKERS

THE WORKERS
PHOTOGRAPHS BY OLIVER STREWE
TEXT BY BLANCHE D'ALPUGET

COLLINS
AUSTRALIA

To the memory of my father, F.G.M.T. Strewe, otherwise known as Odo.

First published in 1987 by William Collins Pty Ltd, Sydney, Australia.

Created and produced by
Modern Times Pty Ltd
P.O. Box 908
Bondi Junction, NSW 2022, Australia

© Photographs Oliver Strewe
© Text Blanche d'Alpuget
© Captions Modern Times Pty Ltd

Designed by Pamela Brewster
Edited by Kirsty Melville
Proof-read by Ella Martin
Typeset in Australia by Deblaere Typesetting
Printed in Hong Kong by Mandarin Offset

National Library of Australia Cataloguing in Publication Data

Strewe, Oliver, 1950-
    The workers.
    ISBN 0 00 217809 5.

    1. Labor and laboring classes – Australia. 2. Labor and laboring classes – Australia – Pictorial works. I. d'Alpuget, Blanche, 1944-   . II. Title.

305.5'6'0994

All rights reserved. No part of this publication may be reproduced, stored in a retrieval system, or transmitted, in any form, or by any means, electronic, mechanical, photocopying, recording or otherwise, without prior permission of the publishers.

This book is sold subject to the conditions that it shall not, by way of trade or otherwise, be lent, re-sold, hired out or otherwise circulated without the publisher's prior consent in any form of binding or cover other than that in which it is published and without a similar condition including this condition being imposed on the subsequent purchaser.

This publication has been partially funded by The Australian Bicentennial Authority to celebrate Australia's Bicentenary in 1988.

CONTENTS

Acknowledgements 7

MAKING A LIVING 9

THE SUGAR 66

DOWN THE MINES 84

IN THE SHEDS 100

WHEAT, COTTON AND CANE 120

ITINERANTS 132

ACKNOWLEDGEMENTS

Blanche d'Alpuget would like to acknowledge the following sources for quotes in the text: Geoffrey Blainey's *The Blainey View*, Macmillan, 1982 for the quote on page 89; G.L. Dasvarma's 'Causes of Death Among Males of Various Occupations' in *Studies in Australian Morality*, edited by N.D. Glashan, University of Tasmania, for the quote on page 89; and Patsy Adam-Smith's *The Shearers*, Nelson, 1982, for the quote on page 108.

Other sources of information were: *The Australian Year Book*, 1985; the Australian Bureau of Statistics for publications on industry and occupation; *The Australian Encyclopaedia*; Patsy Adam-Smith's *Folklore of the Australian Railwaymen*, Seal Books, 1976; Manning Clark's *A Short History of Australia*, Macmillan, 1981; David Moore and Rodney Hall's *Australia, Image of a Nation 1850-1950*, Collins, 1983; Thomas Keneally's *Outback*, Hodder and Stoughton, 1983; Walter Stone's *The World of Henry Lawson*, Paul Hamlyn, 1978; and Eric Hansen for his article, *Low Commotion, A Journey Across the Nullarbor on the Tea and Sugar Train*.

Oliver Strewe would like to thank and acknowledge the following organisations for their assistance:
The Australian Workers' Union, in particular, the General Secretary, G.A. Barr and the State Branch Secretaries – I.R. Cuttler, E.C. Ecob, V.J. Keenan, A.S. Begg, E.J. Butler and E.R. Hodder;
The Community Arts Board and Visual Arts Board of the Australia Council, the Federal Government's arts funding and advisory body; and
the Office of the Minister for the Arts in the New South Wales Government.

He would also like to thank all the organisers of the AWU; with special thanks to Wendy Pymont in the federal office, Susie Scott of the State Library of New South Wales for research, Myles Tomkins of Gulf Helicopters, and Steve Lovasz who kept the Kingswood on the road. All photographs were taken with Nikon cameras and Nikkor lenses.

Above all, Oliver would like to thank those men and women throughout Australia whose photographs were included in this book.

Then hurrah for Australia the golden
When men of all nations now toil
To none will we e're be beholden
Whilst we're able to turn up the soil.
   'The Colonial Minstrel',
     Charles Thatcher, *Hurrah for Australia*

MAKING A LIVING

There are no daily newspapers. There are no TV or radio broadcasts, no cinema, no swimming pool, no shop, no school, no doctor, no church. There is nothing green. There are no trees and the land seems shadowless. Kilometre upon kilometre it rolls away in an everlasting, maddening sameness, like an ocean. The horizon is circular, like the horizon when one is on a ship far from land. For almost 700 kilometres there is no stream or brook or creek and the only vegetation is saltbush and bluebush and grass in the spring which withers before summer. People who get lost here can be beautifully preserved, as mummies.

By day temperatures of more than fifty degrees celsius in the shade will melt the thongs off your feet. At night there is a cool breeze called The Doctor. By 2 am the temperature may have fallen to below freezing – but in a few more hours it will again be too hot to move unless you have to: unless you're a fettler or a navvy tending to the Transcontinental Railway. There are thousands upon thousands of men (and some hundreds of women) who have survived a stint out here on the Nullarbor. They call themselves the Ning-Nongs of the Nullarbor, amused by their own foolhardiness.

Seventy-five years ago building that line – from Port Augusta to Kalgoorlie – was the toughest job in Australia. In 1912 the gangers earned $1.10 a day, lived in tents and ate dry bread, oily butter, salt beef, rice and cabbage. Once a week they got fresh supplies from the 'Tea and Sugar' train; once a week they bathed in a kerosene tin of water and afterwards washed their clothes in the same water.

Some were driven mad by the isolation and hardship. In that circumstance, the solution was to cut your throat.

There were other men who took their wives and children out to the desert in 1912. There was nothing to do in the evenings; for entertainment they would sit around a fire and watch a potato baking in its jacket.

The fettlers and navvies who now maintain the desert railway still depend for their survival on the Tea and Sugar train, but their lives are soft and sweet in comparison to the gangers of 1912-17. In comparison to city workers of 1987, however, they have embraced a life of hardship and self-denial. In moving to the desert they seem like cheerful, wilful people entering religious orders.

Why do they do it?

To be free, they say. For the freedom, the space, the independence, and the dignity which comes from all that.

Out here the hundreds of petty laws regulating city life do not exist – and there are people hiding from justice under assumed names. There are people out here who in a city would not get a job or could not afford housing. There are people out here who love the silence. 'It's the only place in Australia where there is total silence… Your ears ring with it,' one woman said. And there are others, working for Telecom and the Department of Meteorology, who have, for the love of their jobs, accepted an isolated post, and are making the best of it.

Manning Clark has written with disgust that contemporary Australian life is enslaved to a culture of greed and titillation; that consumerism has corrupted the work ethic. He is writing of the many. The people in this book are the few.

These are Australians who work hard and expect little. They prefer to be in a job – any job – than on the dole. Many of those who have gone to the Nullarbor, for example, have done so in preference to living more comfortably, but unemployed.

Some of them are poor, and their children will be poor. They cannot hope, as virtually all Australians have been able to hope since World War II, that their children will be more affluent than they are.

This isolated backcountry lying between the Great Victoria and Gibson deserts in Western Australia, is typical of land where many Australian workers, from the miner to rabbit hunter, fettler to stockman, eke out a living.

THE WORKERS 11

Lunch consists of cold beef and salad sandwiches and a large mug of billy tea for Rod Pickering, Cliff Hughes and Doug Campbell, stockmen at Mittagong Station, a 285,000 hectare property outside Croydon in Queensland's rugged gulf country. 'I'm seventy-five in the shade,' says Doug who was once stranded way out on the station by sudden, torrential rains. He complained, 'I spent ten days on a shirtfull of cold johnnycakes.' Johnnycake: a small flat damper as big as the palm of a hand cooked on the embers of a campfire.

All of them are manual workers of a special category: they work with the earth. 'Humble' and 'humility' are derived from the Latin for 'earth'. The people in these photographs are humble – not in any cringeing Uriah Heap sense of the word, but in its older meaning: they are connected to the earth, grounded within themselves, down-to-earth.

It was in 1984 that Oliver Strewe set out to make a pictorial record of these people. With the help of the Australian Workers' Union, one of Australia's largest unions, he travelled the country photographing Australians at work. The workers pictured here have one thing in common, apart from the hours they put in, they all work with earth-energies.

Their earth-working ranges from the intimacy of underground mining, through many types of agricultural labour. There are the most horrific, bloody farm jobs – mulesing sheep back of Bourke, for example. In one photograph a young man still has gore on his hands from mulesing and his face shows the strain of the work. There are the farm jobs made into art: shearing and creating haystacks, and the jobs of nurturing and preservation, cotton chipping and piglet rearing. The people here live remote from civilisation but they are in the mainstream of the phases of life: creation, preservation, destruction, creation. In the cities, bridge-builders, mainly migrants, also work with earth-energies. They do the bridge formwork: concrete, an earth product, is poured into wooden forms and the men must grade and level it, wash up and be ready for the next pour, working very fast. Bridge building is connecting earth-to-earth. The bridge-builders jobs took them so high that they did not come down all day, even to eat lunch, because descending and ascending would take half their meal break.

For those of us who work in the city, having lunch is an entertainment. For these workers it is an essential refuelling so that they can work on. No doubt there are

'I love my job', said Nancy Sanderson, the animal attendant, at the Commercial Pig Company in Huntley, Victoria where the pig population is over 72,000. Nancy, who has been with the company for fifteen years, looks after the sows and piglets, acting as nurse to the offspring until they are four weeks old. Each month there is a turnover of 1,360 piglets, ten for each sow in the piggery who has given birth.

Knocking off from work is not so easy when you have to descend sixty-five metres before you can go home. Construction workers were forced to reconcile themselves to working in extremely hazardous conditions for the five years it took to build the Gateway Bridge in Brisbane.

THE WORKERS

rural workers who have a beer at lunchtime if there is beer available. But none of the people pictured here drink alcohol during the working day. Their beverages are water or tea.

Australians are one of the most restless peoples in the world, and the most restless Australians are the itinerant labourers of the countryside. Some of them, the fruit pickers who follow the harvest from Queensland to the Victorian Riverina, are so independent of the rest of society that they seem alien. They are not unionised and often their children travel with them and will never or rarely be sent to school. There are other itinerants, the shearers, who are the very archetypes of the male Australian worker. The shearer is adventurous, independent, and an individualist. And above all, he is a mate. It is the shearer who created and from whom the rest of the country has inherited – at least as an ideal – a system of values based on mateship. Travelling through the bush looking for work, walking, riding a horse or a bicycle or a camel, the shearer's survival depended on mutual help, on mates.

The workers pictured here are also that minority of people whose work earns the nation's bread. Agriculture and mining are our foundational industries. As historian Geoffrey Blainey has pointed out: 'We do not fully realise how much the standard of living of nearly every Australian depends on mining.' In 1985-86 Australia's export earnings from mining were $10 billion; agricultural exports earned $6.6 billion; together these two earned sixty per cent of export income. But the people whose work helps earn these billions are less than eight per cent of those employed.

So the people in these pages have another claim upon our attention: they are highly productive. They earn less than city workers and they work longer hours. Farmers work an average of 50.9 hours a week, when the average for all Australian men is 40.2 hours.

Tobacco growing near Myrtleford, Victoria in the fertile valleys below the Australian Alps, is also home to a large Italian community. In preparation for planting the tobacco an Italian worker spends long hours of intense concentration, meticulously ploughing a field.

THE WORKERS 17

Small crop farming can often mean long hours for little financial reward. Hopeful of a good crop, this strawberry farmer, who works just outside Nambour, Queensland, is spraying his patch with insecticide.

Working on the drill of the Bass Strait Oil Rig is one of the hardest, dirtiest, lowest paid jobs on the platform. Here riggers join the drill stem as it pushes down for oil.

But destruction of the work ethic and disillusion about egalitarianism is now so widespread in urban Australia that the typical response to the idea of a book on contemporary Australian workers is: 'Oh – that will be fiction!'

City people, in white collar jobs, like to characterise the Australian worker as a person gazing into the distance while leaning on a shovel. There may be some accuracy in this observation in cities, in jobs paid by the hour. Certainly it is astonishing how much energy city workers have left over at the end of a day. Finding ways to expend that stored-up energy is the obsession of modern city life: what to do in one's leisure hours? How to keep oneself healthy by getting enough exercise? Geoffrey Blainey has calculated that in the 1880s only about three per cent of Australians could sit down during most hours of their daily work. It is the blessing of electricity on the twentieth century that people are *not* tired: until this century the only people who would be awake after ten o'clock at night were the rich, who had done nothing to physically exhaust themselves during the day. But now city people of all classes are so full of beans after dark that they need entertainment – radio, TV, videos, clubs – to continue until morning. In the bush it's a different story. There is no need for pumping iron, jogging, or latenight movies. Work still uses so much energy that by evening people just want to eat, then go to bed.

Shearing, like a lot of agricultural work, is paid for by the 'piece'. Throughout his working day the shearer has had the opportunity to compete against other shearers or himself for speed and excellence. If he wishes, he can turn the whole day into a competitive event, a sports carnival. As Blainey has pointed out, hard work used to be sport in Australia – but now sport is hard work.

The best loved country work-sports were shearing, wood-chopping and cattle branding, and every agricultural show had one or all of these competitions. Here

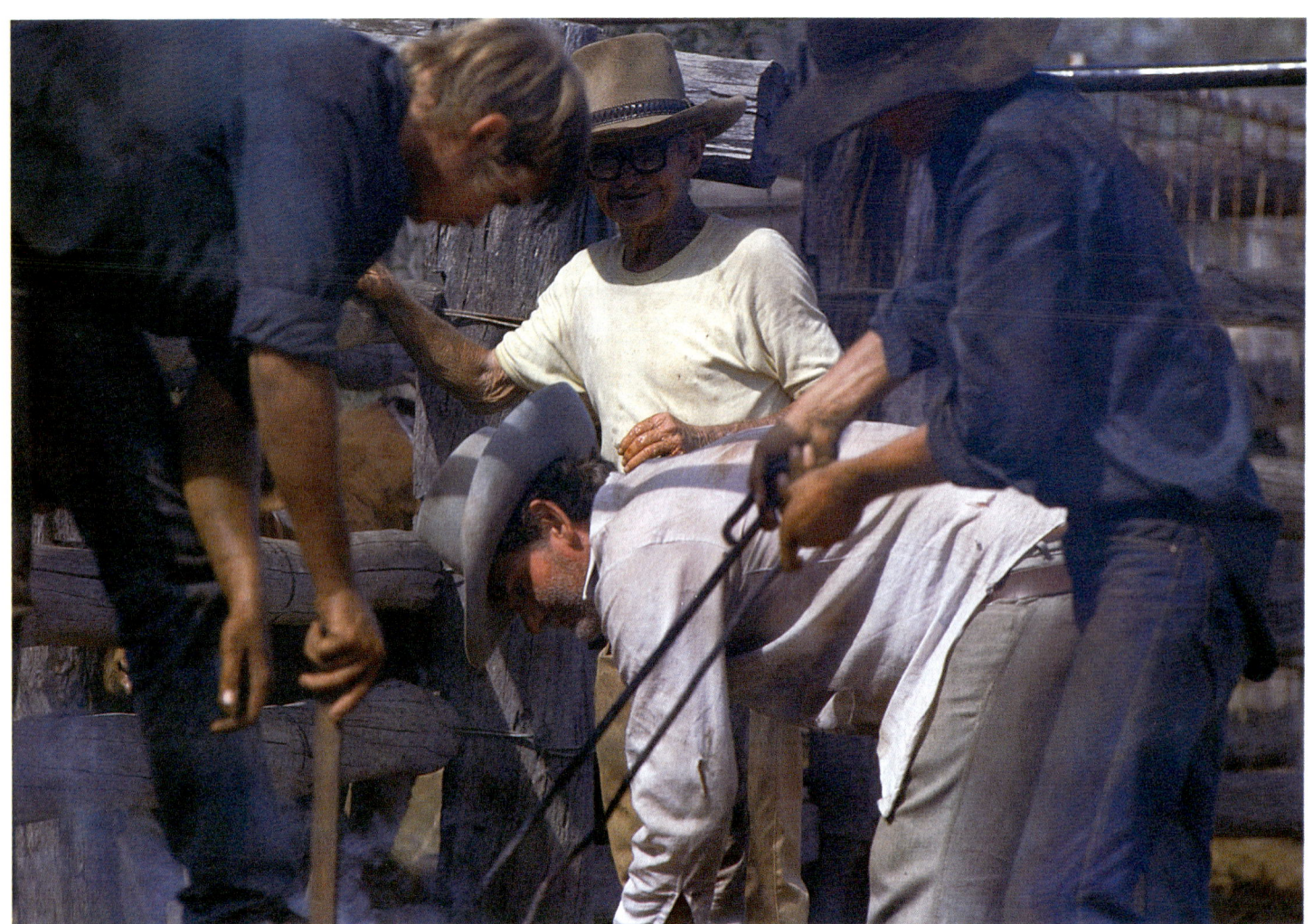

Branding, earmarking and cutting (removing the young bull's testicles for controlling herd quality and fattening) is a recurring job for the stockmen, or 'ringers', during the dry season in Queensland's north. At Mittagong Station, which supports 8,000-10,000 head of Brahmin-cross cattle in the gulf country near Croydon, ringers often work a twelve-hour day, starting at daybreak and finishing around 5.30 pm

Branding is body-bruising work. Here the ringers capture a young bull in a contraption known as a 'cradle', a kind of steel straightjacket, before wrestling it to the ground for branding, cutting and earmarking.

THE WORKERS

was glamorous work, combining skill and intense vitality. Such displays drew huge crowds at the Royal Easter Show in Sydney until the end of the 1960s, when work as sport faded before the novelty of affluence: sport as work.

Until the beginning of World War II Australians were so fascinated by the land and agricultural work that the staff of the respected *Sydney Morning Herald* would move from its offices each Easter to the grounds of the Royal Easter Show, leaving only a skeleton staff at headquarters to report the rest of the news.

From the 1830s to the 1950s Australia rode 'on the sheep's back'. The tail of our shilling coin bore the portrait of a merino ram and there were suggestions in 1927 that the new national capital be called Woolgold. It was gold, discovered first in New South Wales in 1851, that precipitated Australia into nationhood. The goldfields trebled our population, gave us the Eureka Stockade mythology, and produced the Aussie digger, and the digger's slouch hat. Until the 1960s 'Digger' was a common jocular form of address among men; until the 1980s the recognised Australian macho hat was the slouch hat. But myth-making moves with the times: now Australians have again chosen to see themselves idealised in someone who is connected to the soil – not a gold digger or trench warrior, but a crocodile shooter. He wears an Akubra hat.

This broad-brimmed headpiece used to be the symbol of the squatter or the cocky farmer: city-dwelling Australians scorned it as snobbish, or unsophisticated bumpkin gear. Overnight it has been made desirable. On the head of Michael Dundee, Northern Territory crocodile shooter, the Akubra stands for courage, modesty and honour. Michael Dundee is an itinerant. And since the earliest days of the colony the itinerant has been that battler whose insecure, makeshift life is the metaphor for all of human life. Safety in gold and in governments is illusory, this belief says: the race is not to the swift, nor the battle to the strong, neither yet

Left The saddlebag is the stockman's lunchbox. This one, belonging to Aboriginal stockman Reggie Wheeler of Yalko Outstation, carries a corned meat sandwich, tea and sugar, and a quart pot — a tin vessel holding a quart of water for drinking and cooking out on the job.

Above Aboriginal stockmen at Yalko Outstation set out to return some 660 head of Brahmin-cross cattle to their grazing country after testing for tuberculosis. Yalko, a 280,000 hectare property with 10,000-11,000 head of cattle, is part of the Kowanyama Aboriginal Community on the western edge of Queensland's Cape York Peninsula.

THE WORKERS 25

The rabbit shooter is one of the many people who has learnt to make a living on the Nullarbor. The glass is removed from the windows of the hunters' car so that rifles can be easily aimed at their quarry.

bread to the wise, nor yet riches to men of understanding… but time and chance happeneth to them all.

Time and again when Australians make an ideal for themselves they choose the battler, the person who treasures independence and self-reliance, who is resilient in the face of hardship, who *expects* the dice to be loaded, who expects he will have to fight for justice – and accepts that he may not win. It is as if the shock to Europeans encountering this vast dry land, which seemed so occult and hostile, has been permanently imprinted on the national psyche. Australia was a country in which god seemed absent, or dead – or worse, inimical to man. Turning such a place from a dangerous foe into a powerful friend has been the work of building Australia and building Australians. It's not rural people who made Crocodile Dundee a hero, but those of us from the city. The closest that we get to Mother Earth may be lying on our bellies on Bondi Beach, but at some deep level we respond to the sense of living close to the soil and drawing power from it.

There are a few Rabbit Dundees in this book. Since rabbits don't bite these men are not candidates for hero status, although sending the national pest to the big warren in the sky is arguably of greater importance than killing crocs. It is for hard men. The photograph of a blood-crusted car with the glass removed from its windows so that rifles can be aimed through them, speaks about the real life of Australian hunters. Again one sees, along with the unromantic filth, people with a burning desire to be their own masters, to make a living, to be beholden to none. If the welfare state were abolished overnight these men might never know of it. They have accepted insecurity of life and limb and fortune. And technology is unlikely to make them obsolete: we've got rabbits, and that is that.

As for the rest of the Australian landscape, technology blows through it as a gale of creative destruction.

One of Australia's oldest operating hydro-electric plants, the Lake Margaret Power Station on the west coast of Tasmania, is a 'working museum'. It was commissioned in 1914 and its original equipment is still in operation.

First thing every morning Sammy Rogers climbs a 300 metre track to reach the winch house of the Lake Margaret Power Station cable car. There he checks the 'King Billy' pipeline for leaks and makes any needed repairs. Constructed in 1924 of King William pine, the 'King Billy' transports water from Lake Margaret into the power station's generators.

THE WORKERS 29

When wool is cleaned, regraded and baled for export, one of the main by-products is lanolin – a grease that comes from the wool and which is used as a base for creams and cosmetics. Most shearers and wool workers have unusually soft hands because they are in continual contact with the lanolin.

THE WORKERS

According to the census of 1933 more than half a million people, or 19.1 per cent of all those employed then, worked in agriculture. In the nineteenth century the Australian dream had been to own a farm, to be a cocky. By the early twentieth century, a new dream was emerging – urban life, with a brick bungalow of one's own. And the exodus from the countryside was underway. In the 1920s tractors began replacing farm horses, and labour needs were cut by a fourth. In one day a man on a tractor could reap an area that, with horses, took weeks. Harvesting with horses had itself been the technological leap up from the man swinging a scythe. A skilled reaper could scythe half a hectare of wheat in a day. In the 1980s, during harvest time, huge combine tractors chomp through the wheat round-the-clock, gathering half a hectare of grain in minutes. Their drivers sit inside air-conditioned cabins listening to music on headphones.

This sort of farming – noisy, noisesome and boring – offends the sense of beauty based on images of rural work as being 'natural', quiet, somehow feminine and sweet smelling, with more wood than metal in the environment. It may even offend a remnant of religious feeling for the earth, a sentiment that nowadays seems part instinct, part superstition. Demeter, The Mother, was the goddess of wheat and all other cereals. Traditionally she was thanked for her gift of food at harvest time. She still is in the East, where she gives rice. In Indonesia, for example, Demeter is Dewi Sri, the Rice Goddess, and rice must be cut with an implement small enough to fit in the palm of the hand so that Dewi Sri's exquisite sensibilities are not injured by the sight of sharp metal. Australia's efficient mechanical reaping seems raping by comparison.

From the beginning of settlement in the Australian colonies agricultural efficiency has been critical: the land is arid and labour is scarce. And indeed, Australian farmers have a superb record for efficiency: nowhere else in the world has so much dry land been farmed with such success. From the outset Australian farmers have

During harvest time, the workers at Yarral cotton station, on the Wee Waa Road near Narrabri, New South Wales, drive the combine harvesters from daybreak to sundown.

THE WORKERS

At Auscot station in the north-west of New South Wales, where both wheat and cotton are grown, the combine harvesters also operate from early morning until last light.

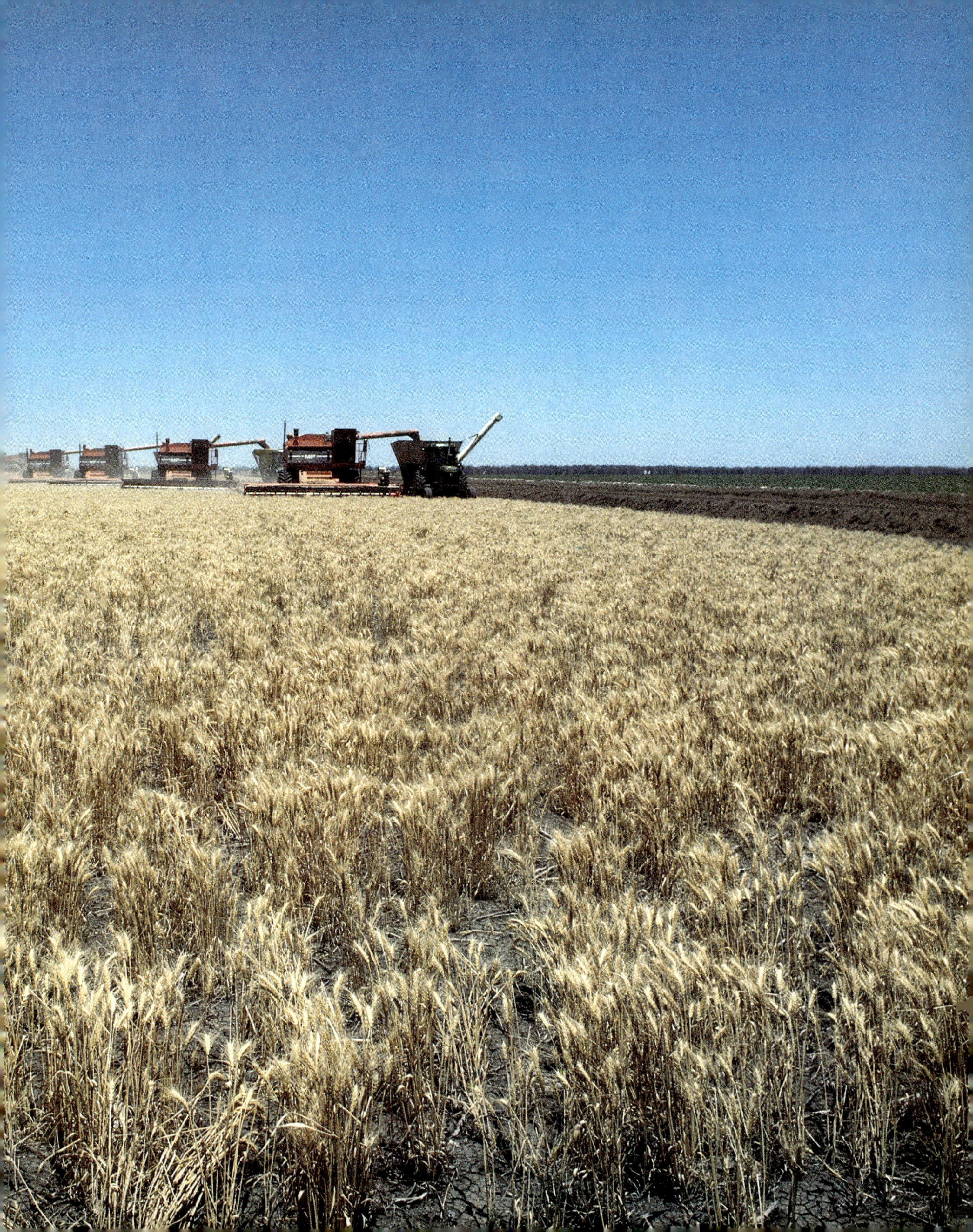

been willing to try new technologies and for a century, until the 1980s, this innovative approach gave Australia, as a food and wool producer, a leading edge in world trade. But inexorably the rest of the world has now caught on to technological and scientific farming. Forty years of peace in Western Europe have allowed it to produce mountains of meat, lakes of milk, pyramids of butter. Miracle rice has brought a green revolution to South-East and East Asia. Famine in Asia, which was a reality in the 1960s, has been made into a nightmare of the past. Man has been practising agriculture, it's believed, for 10,000 years and throughout that time harvest failure leading to famine has haunted him. But in a brilliant effort during the past two decades, after ten millenia, science has defeated famine – or so it seems. Now only the most woebegone backblocks of the world, mostly in Africa, are threatened by starvation from lack of crops.

While this is wonderful for the species Homo Sap, it's not good news for the Aussie cocky. His edge of higher productivity is continuously eroded and his markets are under threat. To stay in business he must continue to reap the whirlwind of technological change and opportunity.

In 1900 there were 3.6 million hectares of land put to agriculture in Australia and about thirty per cent of employed people worked on the land. By 1960 there were 10.6 million hectares being farmed. The census of 1961 found that only 10.1 per cent of those in employment worked in agriculture. By 1984, 21 million hectares of Australia were put to crops and animals. The census of 1981 revealed that only 5.5 per cent of all employed people worked the land. So, while the national farm was doubled in size in twenty-five years, the numbers of those labouring on it were almost halved.

The shrinking process continues. By the end of this century many of the occupations depicted in these pages will no longer exist. Manual asparagus cutting, for

The days are long gone when a labourer would take his canvas water bag to work. In the asparagus fields near Cowra, the canvas has been replaced by polystyrene.

When asparagus has been harvested, it is placed in bundles ready to be collected and stacked in wooden box-like carts drawn by draught horses. All the asparagus grown near Cowra is sent to the Edgell factory which cans 2200 tonnes each year.

THE WORKERS 37

A 'cut in the hill' is the term used to describe the harvesting of asparagus. A chisel-type knife is thrust into the side of the furrow cutting the plant under the ground, then jerked downwards. This chops off the base of the asparagus causing the upper part of the plant to pop up. At the height of the harvesting season – through September and October – about ninety cutters work the fields near Cowra in New South Wales.

example, is already on the extinction list, along with the succulent white variety of asparagus which must be cut manually. A green variety, growing above ground, is easier to cut than the more tender, pale underground shoots. A skilled cutter can earn $900 a week for a thirteen week season, but the technique is difficult and few are attracted to learning it: an unskilled cutter may earn as little as $4 a day until he or she becomes proficient — and who can live on $4 a day? The asparagus industry in Australia seemed as if it would die from lack of labour before the introduction of the tougher, green asparagus and mechanical harvesting. At Cowra in New South Wales we can still watch horses with hoofs like dinner plates walking slowly along the rows of asparagus mounds, pausing for bunches of already cut stalks to be gathered up. But already in nearby fields there are dinky little vehicles carrying six or eight women who cut and gather the asparagus in one operation. The asparagus horse will be a zoo animal within a couple of years.

Nuts and grapes have been picked mechanically for decades and nowhere in the land do buxom girls hold their skirts up to their hips as they trample down the vintage. Such suggestive and unhygienic practices may still exist in poor parts of Europe, but they are not for us. We crush our grapes mechanically. In another decade there may be a machine for picking citrus and soft fruit and the gangs of itinerant pickers will vanish. Concrete sleepers are being laid across the Nullarbor, replacing wooden railway sleepers, which, for seventy years, have been a delicacy for termites. The work of the railway navvy is being abolished along with the termite's dinner.

In the countryside north of Wagga Wagga, in the Coolamon-Matong-Ganmain area of New South Wales, haystacks shaped like giant farmhouse loaves dot the landscape. Once all farmers built their own haystacks. But the secrets of the craft now belong to a few local stack builders and their teams. Sheaf hay is disappearing from Australia and with it, the stack builder. The area north of Wagga is now the

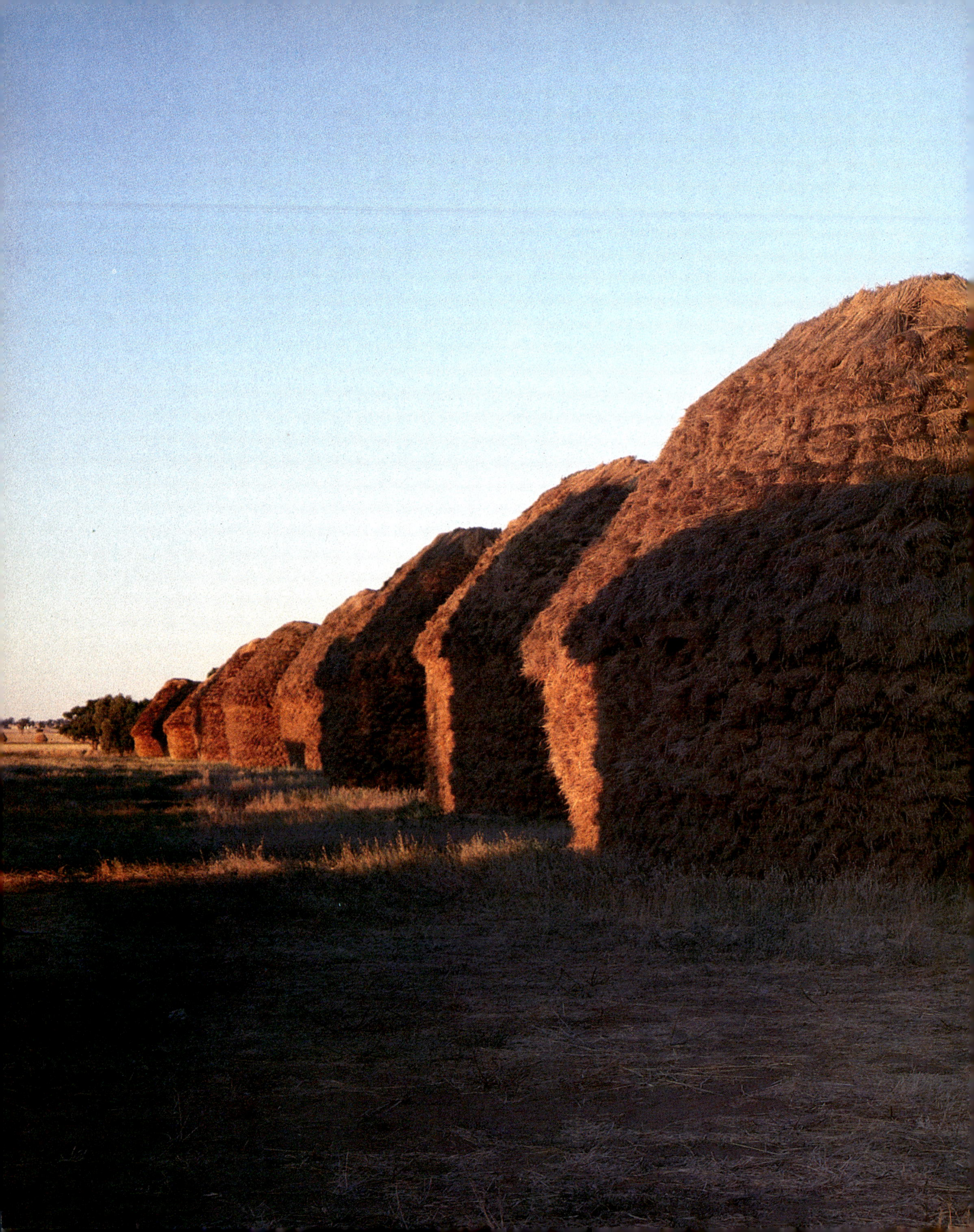

Built without nails, wire or planks, traditional haystacks are fast disappearing. In the Riverina, around Coolamon, Matong and Ganmain a few local stack builders still continue the age-old craft.

THE WORKERS 41

Traditional craftsmen say, 'if a stack is not stooked right, it just won't stand up'. A stook consists of between twelve and twenty sheaves of wheat or oats which stand in the paddock for a week to dry before being gathered. Each stook is then collected by a horsedrawn wagon and taken to the foot of an elevator. The lorry pitcher, as he is called, then pitchforks individual sheaves onto the elevator.

The stack pitcher, standing at the top of the elevator, forks the sheaf to the turner before it falls onto the stack. The turner then places the sheaf either right side up or down for the builder who puts it in its final position.

THE WORKERS 43

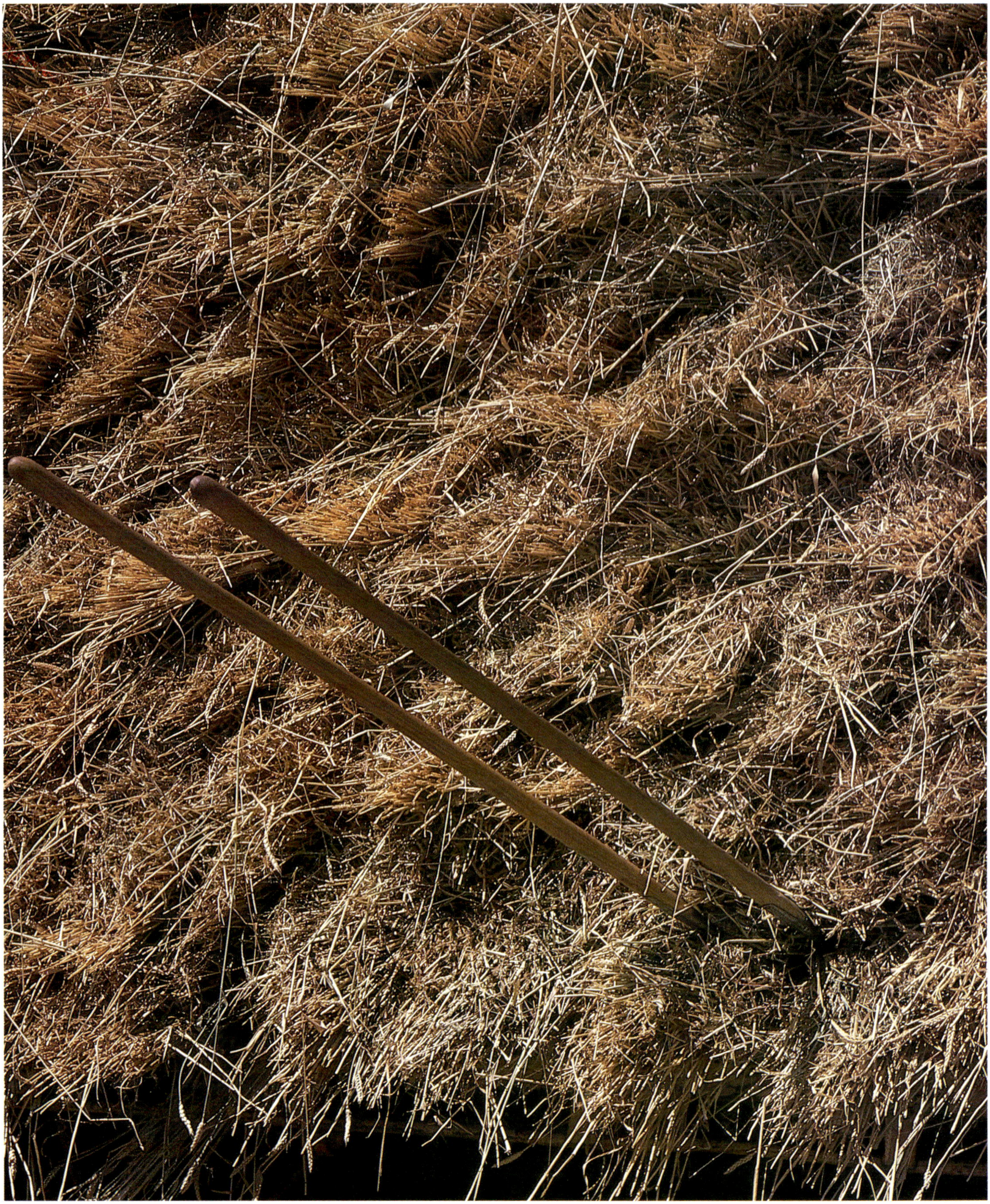

Pitchforks are used to pick up stooks in the paddock and later to unload them at the stack site. Once the truck is loaded they are planted firmly into the hay.

The builder is the craftsman, the only person who can monitor the construction of a stack. He puts the bundle of hay in its final place, forking, positioning and pressing every sheaf in the stack.

only thriving hay district left, and in the past decade only three men have learned the difficult craft of stack-building.

A good haystack must be able to stand in wind and rain for five years without deteriorating. In the end it will be eaten by racehorses, as chaff, but meanwhile it must have a strong heart and waterproof roof. When half-built it must be so springy that, if a person jumps on one end of it, the other end will rear up like a wave. The stack-builder pictured here is so used to the curiosity his work arouses that he carries a visitors' book in his car. When people driving past stop to ask him questions about building haystacks he asks them to sign his book. But these beautiful golden shapes, which could have been painted by Monet, or Gauguin before he went to Tahiti, will in all likelihood have vanished by the end of the century, along with the fine craftsman and his book of names.

Robots may replace hard-rock miners in the twenty-first century. Sheep-breeding experiments aim to produce an animal which can be peeled of its fleece.

A banana-merino would spell the end of Australia's proudest worker, the shearer. Such a sheep sounds grotesque in 1987, but almost all farm animals are misshapen monsters when compared to their wild ancestors, and the merino itself is already a ridiculous creature adapted to converting small quantities of grass into such large quantities of greasy wool that it falls over and dies if it is not regularly shorn.

While geneticists struggle with peelable sheep, in the meantime they have invented the Wonderland White Rabbit. These rabbits, immune to disease and weighing about ten kilograms, will be farmed in the Broken Hill area from 1987. They will be immune to myxomatosis. Super bunnies are a scientific marvel we may live to regret. Already New South Wales farmers have raised cries of alarm against these big white rabbits: if they escape from their high-security, high-tech

Driven by poor work opportunities at home, Torres Strait Islanders have become renown as fettlers on the railways of Australia. They, together with Polish Australians, make up the majority of fettlers on the Hammersley Iron Line. Known locally as the 'H.I. Line', it forms the vital link between the Tom Price mine and the port of Dampier in the isolated north-west of Western Australia. Perhaps the extremes of their respective home environments makes them able to adapt to the harshness of Australia's north west.

THE WORKERS 47

Replacing the original wooden sleepers with concrete ones on the H.I. Line between the Tom Price mine and Dampier is a particularly arduous task, as the inscription on the track shows. Their job is made doubly difficult by the fact that the gang has to completely dismantle its machinery and rejoin the line everytime the iron ore train comes through.

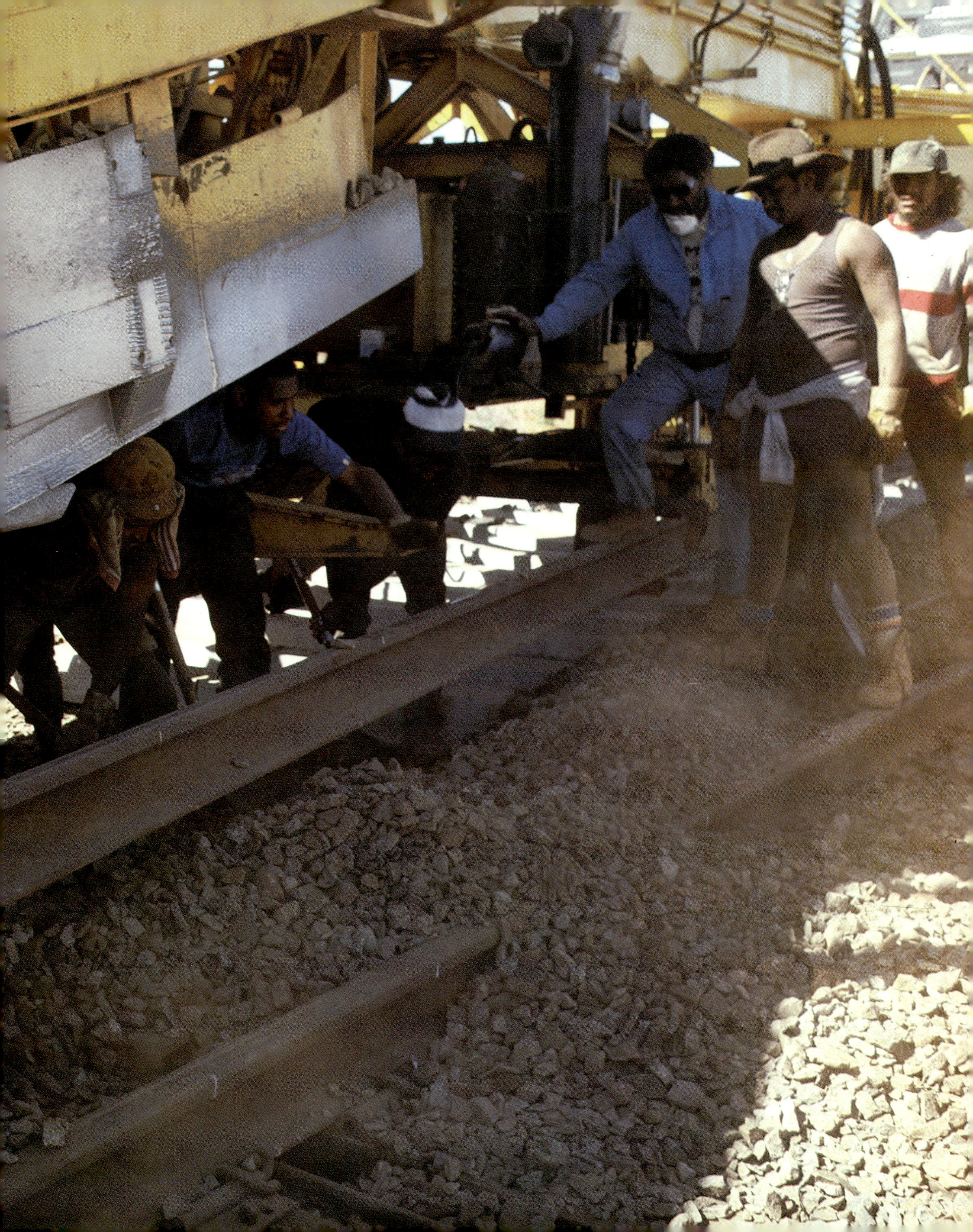

Concrete ganger on
the Hammersley Iron
Line.

Women truck drivers in the Pilbara region in Western Australia's north-west, take equal place alongside their male counterparts on the giant 'Haulpaks'. These trucks, which transport the iron ore to the crusher at the Pannawonica Mine, each carries 120 tonnes.

THE WORKERS

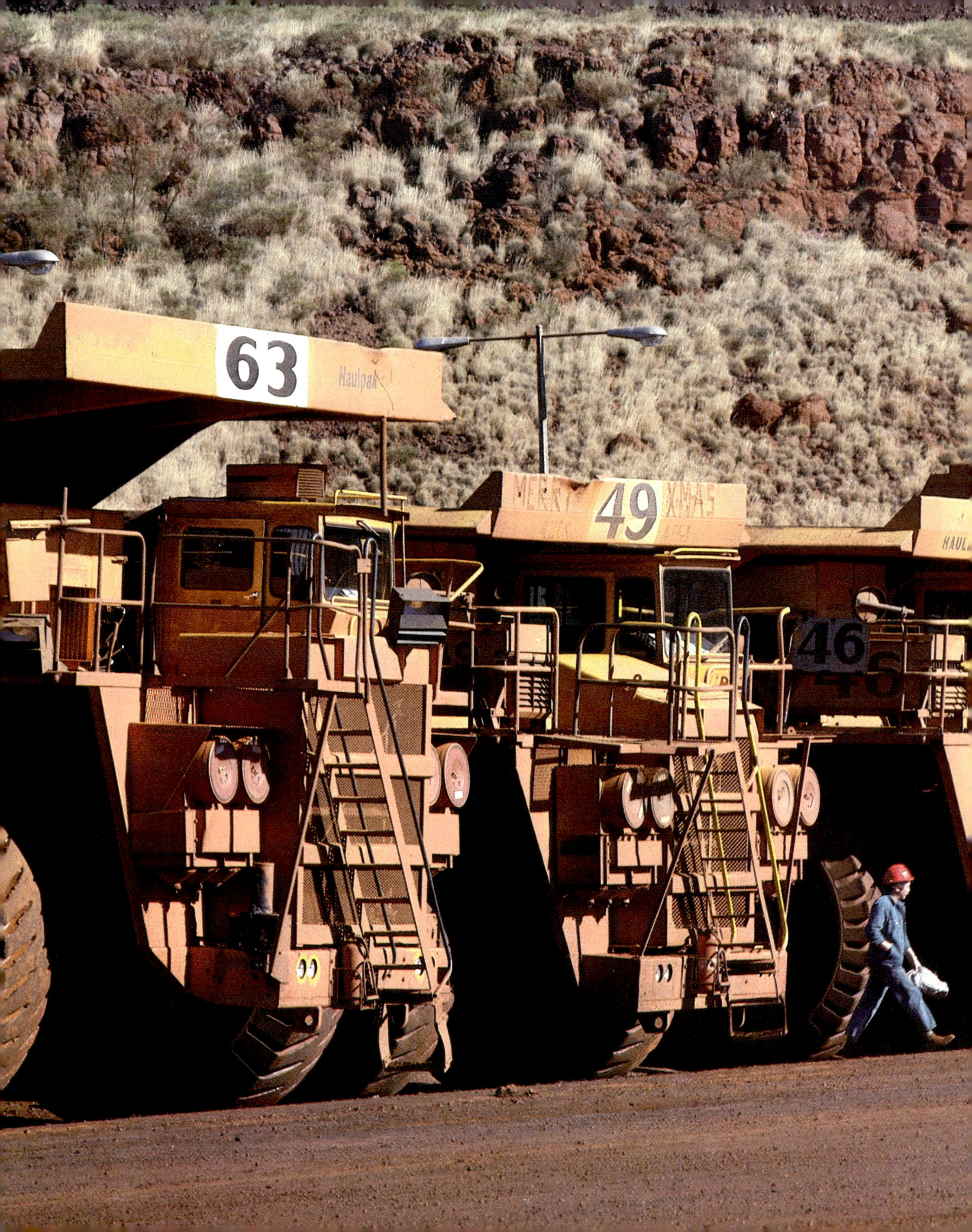
63
Haulpak
49
46

The 'Haulpaks' used in the Pilbara, are so enormous that a ladder is built onto the truck so the driver can climb into the cabin. There are three 8-hour shifts at Pannawonica, operating six days of the week, and two on Sunday. The countryside in this area is so harsh and dry that roads have to be watered to keep dust levels down in order for trucks to keep on the move.

THE WORKERS 53

The cook at Kalkaroo Station, west of the Darling River in New South Wales, has to cater for all meals and smoke-ohs (tea breaks), seven days a week. This means feeding all the shearers, rouseabouts, press operator and contractor, and sometimes the station hands as well.

farmyards, the country could be faced with its most desperate rabbit plague. And Rabbit Dundee could be the hero of 2001.

As technology continues to remove jobs and dump machines in the place of people the agricultural workforce not only shrinks year by year, its nature changes from overwhelmingly male to largely male. Since the 1970s refinements in technology have brought women into agricultural work in large numbers. There were 72,000 women working as farmers in the mid-1970s. Ten years later there were 106,000 of them. Yet in the same period the number of farming males decreased from 355,000 to 349,000.

Muscles and a willingness to take a physical battering from work have probably been the most important elements in the past success in Australian agriculture. Today machines have removed the importance of brawn and much of the wear-and-tear that farm work imposes on human flesh (compare reaping by scythe to reaping with a combine harvester; in the absence of horses, men were yoked to the plough as draught animals). And this has enabled more women to enter areas of work traditionally left to men. Not that women haven't endured the rigours of life on the farm over the years. In *The Drover's Wife* Henry Lawson wonderfully captures a woman's response to the harshness and isolation of life in the Australian bush. The drover's wife waits, imprisoned at home with her children and a yellow-eyed dog, threatened by bushfires, bulls and a maurauding black snake. She sits up all night waiting for her chance to kill it.

The qualities of moral courage and reliability which Lawson saw in his country woman are revealing themselves afresh as farmers' wives and daughters leave their houses – from choice or from economic necessity – to work in the sunshine. They are able to do so because of technology: technology in the field, and technology in the kitchen which has transformed the farm kitchen from a small factory where

A ferry operator on the Sackville ferry which crosses the Hawkesbury River in New South Wales, Evelyn Bolas, considers her job a way of life. She works seven days a week: from 4 pm to midnight on weekdays, and from 8 am to 4 pm on weekends. It is hard physical work.

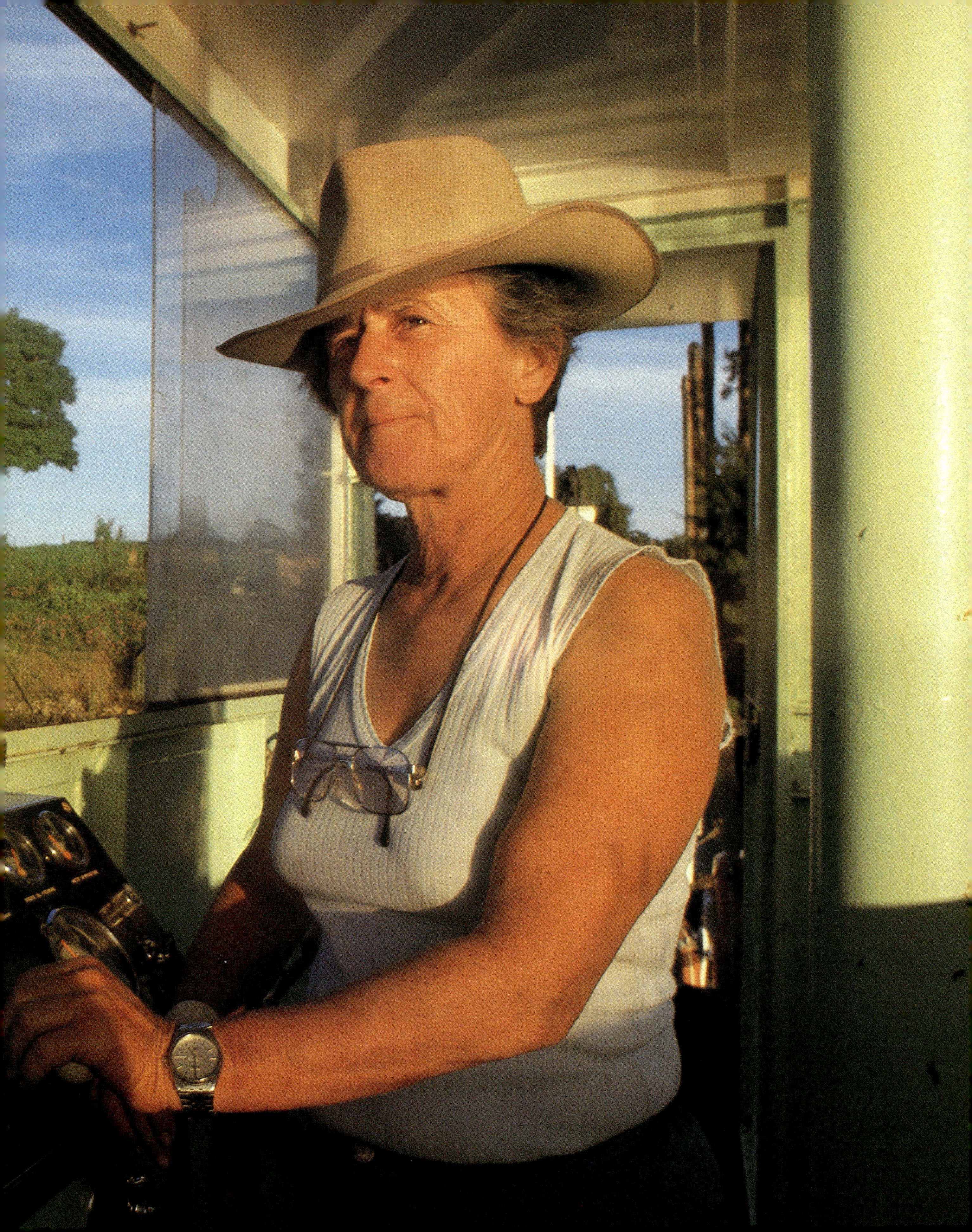

There are twenty-three horses at the Warbett Lodge stables where Tanya Wolfer is a strapper for Betty Lane, one of Australia's first women trainers. On race days, in addition to her normal chores of feeding and grooming the horses, and cleaning their stables, she has to prepare the horses that are running.

preserves were bottled, meat was smoked, bread baked and butter churned, into a space where meals are quickly prepared and the dishes washed afterwards, with a bit of luck, by a Lady Chef.

So far women make up fewer than one-third of all agricultural workers, but the trend towards equality of numbers in rural employment continues. 'There is no worker more reliable than the Australian woman,' according to Bluey Rodwell, an Australian Workers' Union organiser. 'You never find her, when paid by the hour, lying down or off looking for a bit of shade.' This reputation for trustworthiness is likely to open more opportunities for paid work for women in country districts. It is even possible that technological change may reverse the gender mix. A book of photographs published next century about Australians who work intimately with the earth may show just a few male faces among the many female ones.

While we lament that skills are lost, that scientific horticulture pollutes with insecticides and herbicides and that noisy, smelly mechanised farming is as uninspiring as production-line work, there is no turning back. We are, as it were, sailing across the Pacific: we cannot jump overboard and swim the rest of the way. As the industrial revolution has shown, the solution to the problems created by machinery is not to dispense with the machines, but to improve them. Bad farming has created deserts: the Harappan Desert of Pakistan, deserts in north and east Africa and, forty years ago, dust-bowls in south-central parts of the United States, the land of *The Grapes of Wrath*. These disasters were caused by unsound and bad husbandry, and primitive technology. Destroying the world's rainforests, as has happened in Australia, and thereby countless species of flora and fauna is criminally bad husbandry. It, too, needs only the most primitive technology to do its damage. Thoughtless clearing of the land, resulting in soil erosion, is the greatest threat to Australian agriculture. According to the Bible, man, while allowed dominion over fish and fowl and every living thing, is accountable to God for the good management of the earth.

Workers and their machinery are made to look insignificant by the immensity of this 120 metre high dam wall on the Lower Pieman River in Tasmania's west. The Pieman River project will produce 1,700 million units of electrical energy annually and has taken workers twelve years to complete.

A dwarf labourer shows considerable enterprise by standing on a bucket to pour concrete at the Lower Pieman Dam construction site on the west coast of Tasmania.

Some environmentalists fear that science and technology will so disturb the balance of nature that generations to come will see in springtime only a blackened face. The acid rain that is destroying the forests of the northern hemisphere seems the herald of such a future. But while this is nature's response to human meddling with the system on one front, on another she reacts with staggering generosity, putting forth crops and flocks in abundance as her answer to high-tech and scientific methods of agriculture.

In a country as young to agriculture as Australia it is within living memory for many to have seen the bush turned into pasture, wilderness into wheatfields. Urban people tend to think of the nation's history as a parade of political actions – mostly, decisions to go to war. But the oldest Australians, surveying the continent through the experience of at least 47,000 years of occupation, know otherwise. For them, the arrival of the white man was the appearance in the garden of an irresistible serpent. He wore a strange second skin that he could shed at will, like a snake, and with his cunning devices he immediately set to work destroying their garden to make one of his own design.

Certainly the gun and the leg iron have played a part in the subjugation of Aboriginal people. But it was the plough and the shovel that stole the land. Agriculture has been at least as significant as violence in destroying Aboriginal life.

The original Australians belonged to the land, the land did not belong to them. But now it belongs to us, and we are challenged to learn how to belong to it: to respond, to adapt ourselves, and to respect as well as to exploit and redesign.

Workers wear thigh-high waders to take measurements in the briny salt fields at Dampier Salt in the north-west of Western Australia. Dampier Salt is one of Australia's largest solar salt producers. Continual sunshine and low rainfall at Dampier Salt makes for rapid evaporation of the sea water. The remaining salt ends up in huge mounds which are then washed and stored before being loaded onto trucks for export. The salt produced is used industrially or exported to Japan.

THE WORKERS

A family picnic by the sea at Dampier, and not a tree in sight.

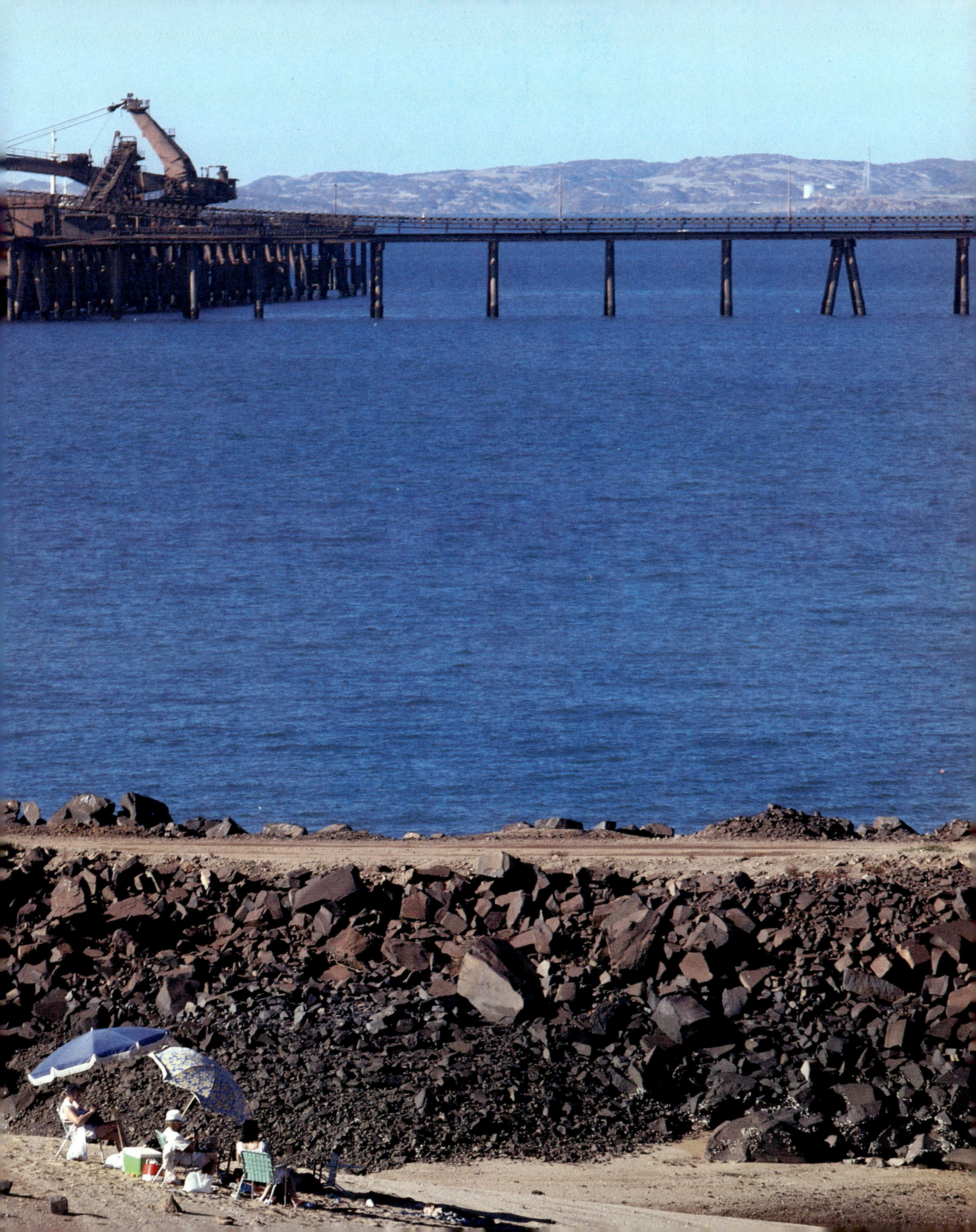

THE SUGAR

The Nullarbor is shadowless, like something which does not quite exist; a dream. By day, its sky is an immense blueness without clouds, and by night a frozen firework of stars. Its earth is a foot of red soil covering limestone. Across this forbidding, hypnotic landscape the single line of the Transcontinental Railway travels straight as an arrow, the longest straight stretch of line in the world.

The Desert Railway, as the Transcontinental was called, was built during World War I as one of the greatest engineering feats of the age. A labour force of 3500 men and hundreds of horses, donkeys and camels had to be accommodated in the country without food, shelter or amenities. From Port Augusta to Kalgoorlie, a distance of 1684 kilometres, there is not a single running stream. For almost a third of this expanse, the 676 kilometres of the Nullarbor, there is not a single tree. Temperatures range from minus five to more than fifty degrees celsius, causing the rails to buckle wildly. Artesian bore water is so salty that it must be desalinated to make it fit for human and animal consumption. But 'fit for' is often relative: the men who built the Desert Railway lived in conditions which, nowadays, would be an outrage of International Labour Organisation conventions. One camp of 300 men was built in a hollow, without sanitation, and made such a stink that it could be smelled for miles. There were such swarms of flies in it that when the Tea and Sugar train arrived the butcher who travelled on it could barely see to cut his meat. Without ice in the camps meat had to be eaten immediately; the dry air turned bread into stones within twenty-four hours. As the time grew closer for the arrival of the Tea and Sugar, the gangers' camps were reduced to damper for food.

'The Sugar' still runs once a week from Port Augusta to Kalgoorlie, bringing food, drink, mail, pay and videos to the settlements dotted every 200 kilometres along the track. A settlement is five to six neat, cream-painted clapboard cottages, each with a fence and a front gate and around them: nothing. The fettlers and their families and the concrete gang — a gang of pick and shovel workers which is replacing the Transcontinental's 2.5 million jarrah sleepers with concrete ones – have learned to live without. They have their nightly cool breeze, The Doctor, and each other. It is said that the Nullarbor grapevine is the fastest in the world. Any trouble causes a chain reaction right along the line as the fettlers take sides. The entire length of the track can be thought of as an immmensely long, thin village, where scandal and gossip runs from tongue to tongue as fast as it does in a newspaper office.

There is general excitement once a week when The Sugar is due. Handfuls of people gather at the railheads looking at their watches: The Sugar is early. The Sugar is late.

They have appeared suddenly. Most of them are residents of the cottages and have walked a few metres, others have driven 200 kilometres and arrive in clouds of grit, driving battered, unregistered cars. There are hunters – rabbits, fox, wild cat – who have knocked the windows from their vehicles so they can shoot through them. Other hunters arrive in dusty jeeps festooned with furry corpses. A feral catskin fetches $10. A pair of rabbits sells for $1.20 and a successful hunter shoots 150 to 200 pairs a night. The contractor for a rabbiting gang arrives at the train line with a wheelbarrow to buy stores for the week. Some Commonwealth policemen who guard the perimeter of Maralinga turn up, clean and spruce, each one with a radioactive sensor pinned to his shorts. Sometimes a couple of trucks arrive from the Oak Valley Aboriginal community near Maralinga. One truck will be loaded with drums of petrol from The Sugar, the other with water from the train's water gin. Oak Valley has its own bore water, not too salty to drink, but radioactive.

If The Sugar is late it could be a dust storm; or ants, or grasshoppers. These insects, in swarms, can make the rails so slippery on an incline that the wheels loose traction. The Sugar is fitted with automatic sanders but even they have not been

The Tea and Sugar train runs weekly across the Nullarbor Plain, between Port Augusta and Kalgoorlie, to service the fettlers and tiny hamlets on the Transcontinental Railway. Australian Workers' Union organiser, Ray McDonald, travels on 'The Sugar' four times a year, holding union meetings which often consist of a mere tiny gathering of track workers and their families beside the railway line.

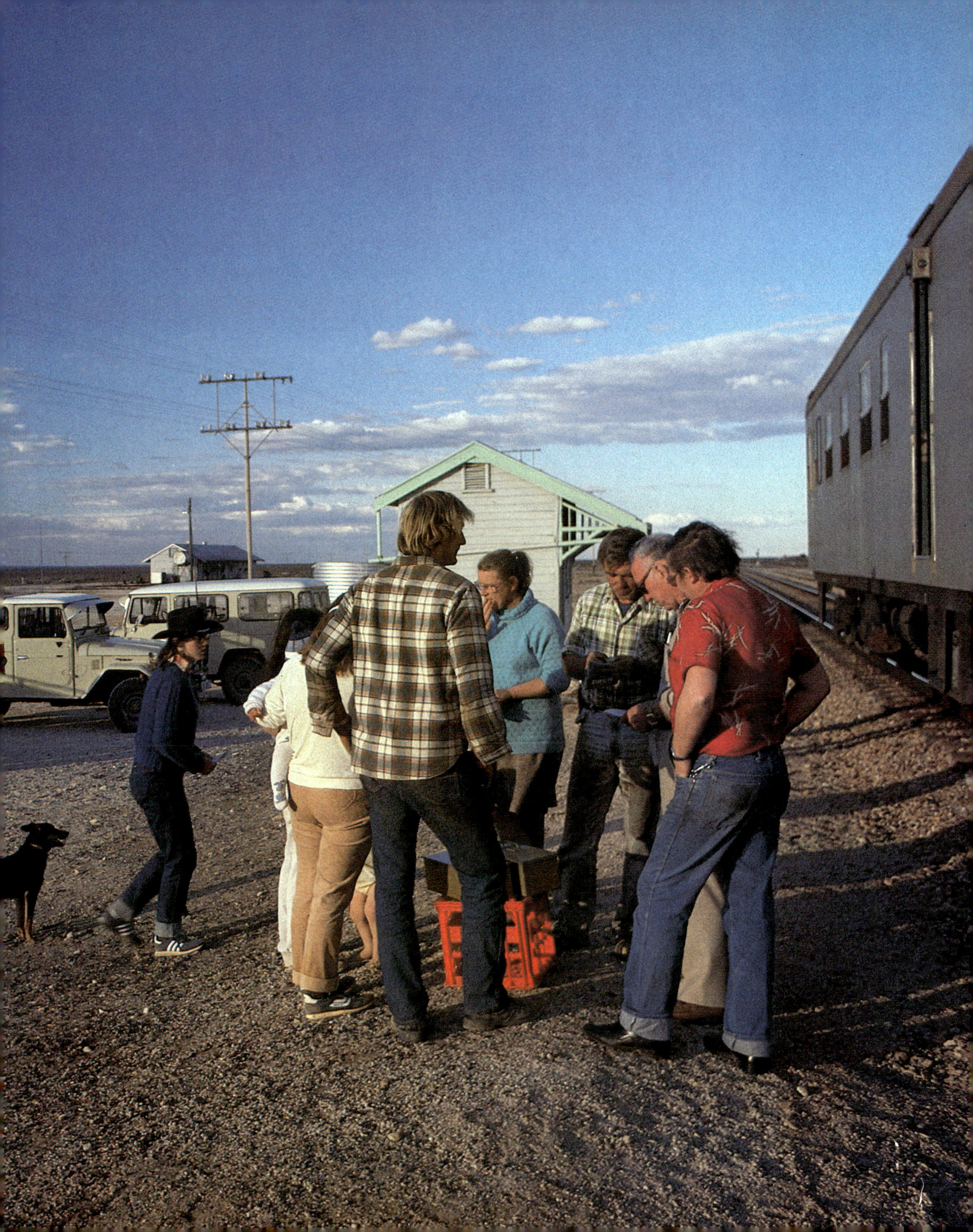

Fettlers on the Nullarbor, like this man at Stirling North in South Australia, have to endure extremes of temperature, ranging from fifty degrees celsius to below freezing, throughout the year.

One of the first fettler camps on the Nullarbor Plain, Watson, is home to this fettler and his wife. Most fettlers and their families only stay for about a year out on the Nullarbor Plain, the extreme isolation and harsh living conditions eventually taking their toll.

THE WORKERS 71

enough to keep the train going through a huge swarm. To be stopped by ants is sickening for the drivers and guards, for in the still, hot air they choke on the stench of formic acid.

People fret. And then, boring a hole through the seamless wall of earth and sky, the train comes into view. The mood turns festive. Soon there will be cuts of meat ordered from Port Augusta, Papa Guiseppi's frozen pizzas, paddle-pops for the kids, magazines, cartons of beer, letters and fresh vegetables. By the end of the run the vegetables that remain are almost dead and there is almost nothing leafy and green but the stalwart cabbage.

Once a fortnight the mailroom on the train also serves as pay wagon for the fettlers, whose after-tax basic pay is $250 per week. The train stops long enough for everyone to do their shopping, collect and post their mail, swap videos, have a chat with the driver and guards – and then it's off to the next settlement.

One of the most remarkable of the people who live beside the Transcontinental is Ziggy Wieczorek, now close to retirement after forty years working for the railways. He was born in Poland. When he arrived in Australia in 1948 he headed for the bush, seeking peace, steady work and to be as far as possible from the madding crowd. Few fettlers spend more than a year working on the Nullarbor line; Ziggy has tended it for decades. Once every five years he treats himself to a trip to Adelaide where he walks in the public gardens and visits the zoo – for his great love, besides solitude, is animals. He lives with five large dogs on the outskirts of Barton (population: 15), as a semi-hermit.

Like other railway workers Ziggy is provided with a house, but he chooses not to stay in it. Instead he has built himself a compound on a sandhill, neatly fenced, and floored with hundreds of old timber sleepers. There are two beds: one his, the

The oldest fettler on the Barton section of the line, Ziggy Wieczorek has been working for the railways for nearly forty years. Today he feels more at home with his five dogs in Barton than in the city or in his native Poland.

THE WORKERS

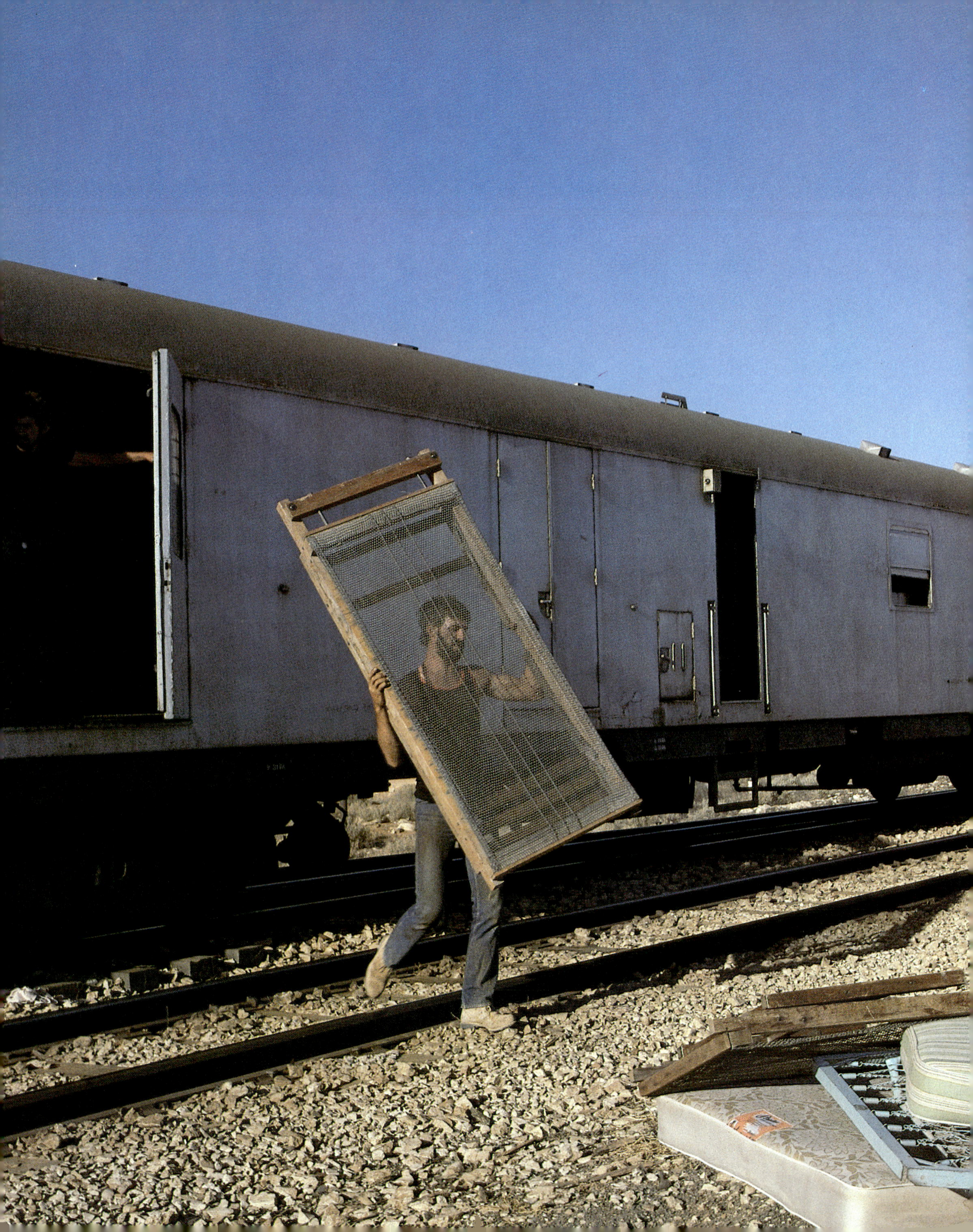

The Sugar is the lifeblood of the tiny communities scattered along the Transcontinental line. Everything is brought in on The Sugar.

THE WORKERS 75

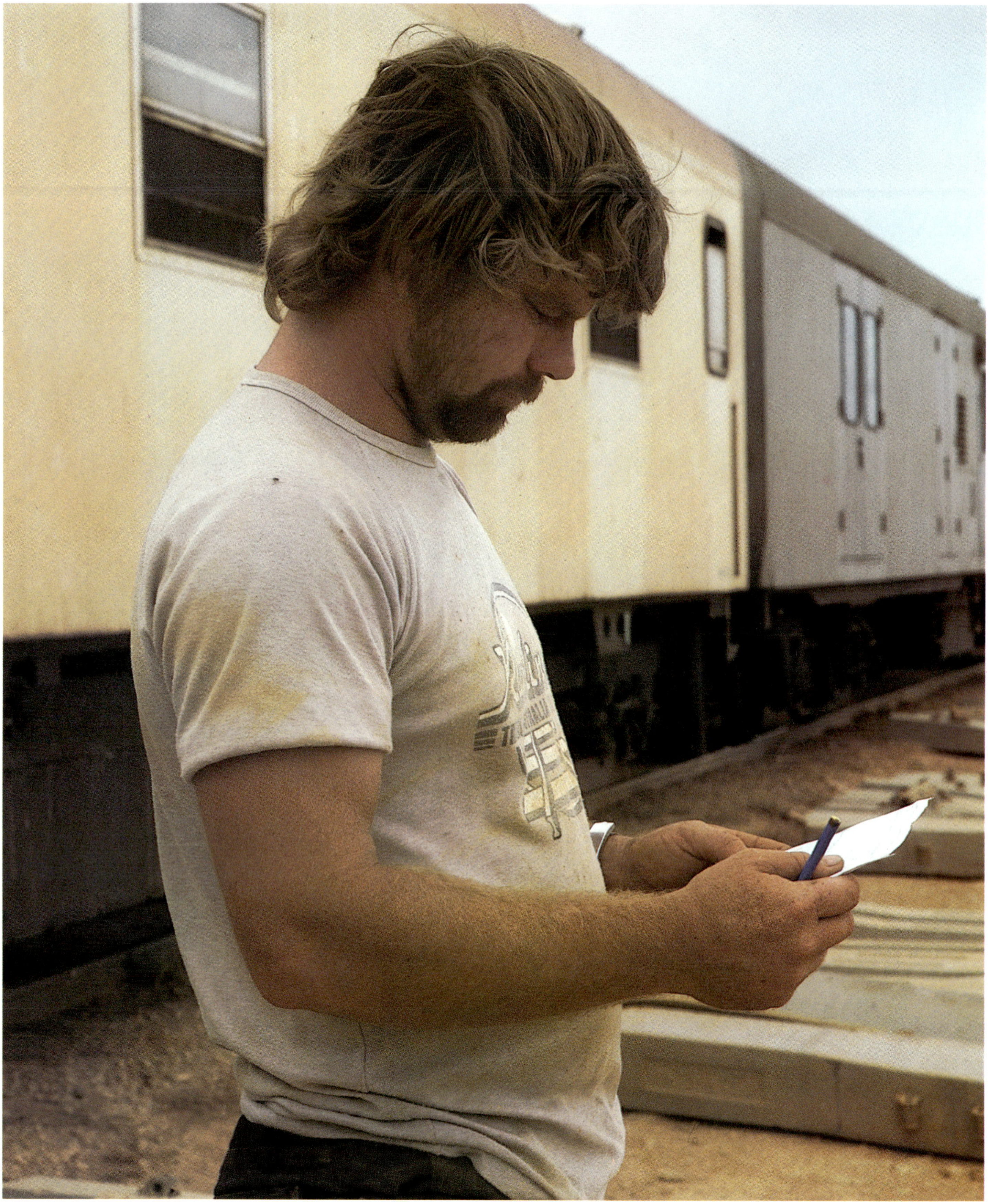

Every second week a post office and bank van with a paymaster are attached to The Sugar.

The heart of the Tea and Sugar train today is the mini-supermarket van, complete with check-outs, shopping baskets and plastic carry-bags. In days gone by the train used to carry livestock and a butcher who would cut meat to order.

THE WORKERS 77

other the dogs'. All this is visible from the train. But Ziggy is concerned about privacy and has been known to throw things at people who stare at his curious dwelling.

He chooses to live away from the world, but not disconnected from it. After the NASA space shuttle disaster, which he had been following on his shortwave radio, Ziggy remarked laconically, 'You can drive a second-hand motorcar. You can't drive a second-hand spacecar'. The harshness of the environment does not oppress him. 'I have freedom here,' he said.

Another man, who, at the end of World War II, sought a hermit life in the bush, is Bill Savage. An octogenarian, he lives at the western end of the Nullarbor line, some thirty-five kilometres from the railway track, up a path imprinted with wild camel spoor. Around him is what is left of a sandalwood forest. Western Australia and the Northern Territory used to export a huge quantity of sandalwood to China, for incense, but the few sandalwood trees left in Australia now are protected. Bill began collecting sandalwood in the 1930s and after war service returned to snigging sandalwood roots and stumps. He had then and drives still a 1929 Longbed Chevrolet truck, a fantastic skinny-wheeled insect-looking vehicle, as patched as a boxer's eyebrow, its front bumperbar made from a large log and its radiator protected by a screen of thick wire mesh. Bill has a contract with the Australian Sandalwood Company in Fremantle to which he supplies fifty tonnes of wood annually, earning $600 a tonne. He is one of the last licensed sandalwood collectors left in the country, and certainly the oldest. At eighty-three Bill moves a little slowly but his peaceful face and his strong body are an advertisement for an outdoor life, a vegetarian diet – and no alcohol or tobacco.

Bill's house is a tent, an antique like his truck, tattered and torn and patched, and very friendly looking. He rises at dawn each day, handgrinds wheat for a bowl of

A resident of the Nullarbor for over forty years, Bill Savage, a sandalwood collector, lives some thirty-five kilometres up a dusty track from Karonie. In the background is Bill's old truck – a 1929 Longbed Chevrolet – which he has been using since 1946.

THE WORKERS

Bill Savage snigs the sandalwood roots and stumps with a chain hitched to the back of his truck, then cleans them by hand with an axe. His sandalwood sells for $600 a tonne, most of it ending up as Chinese incense.

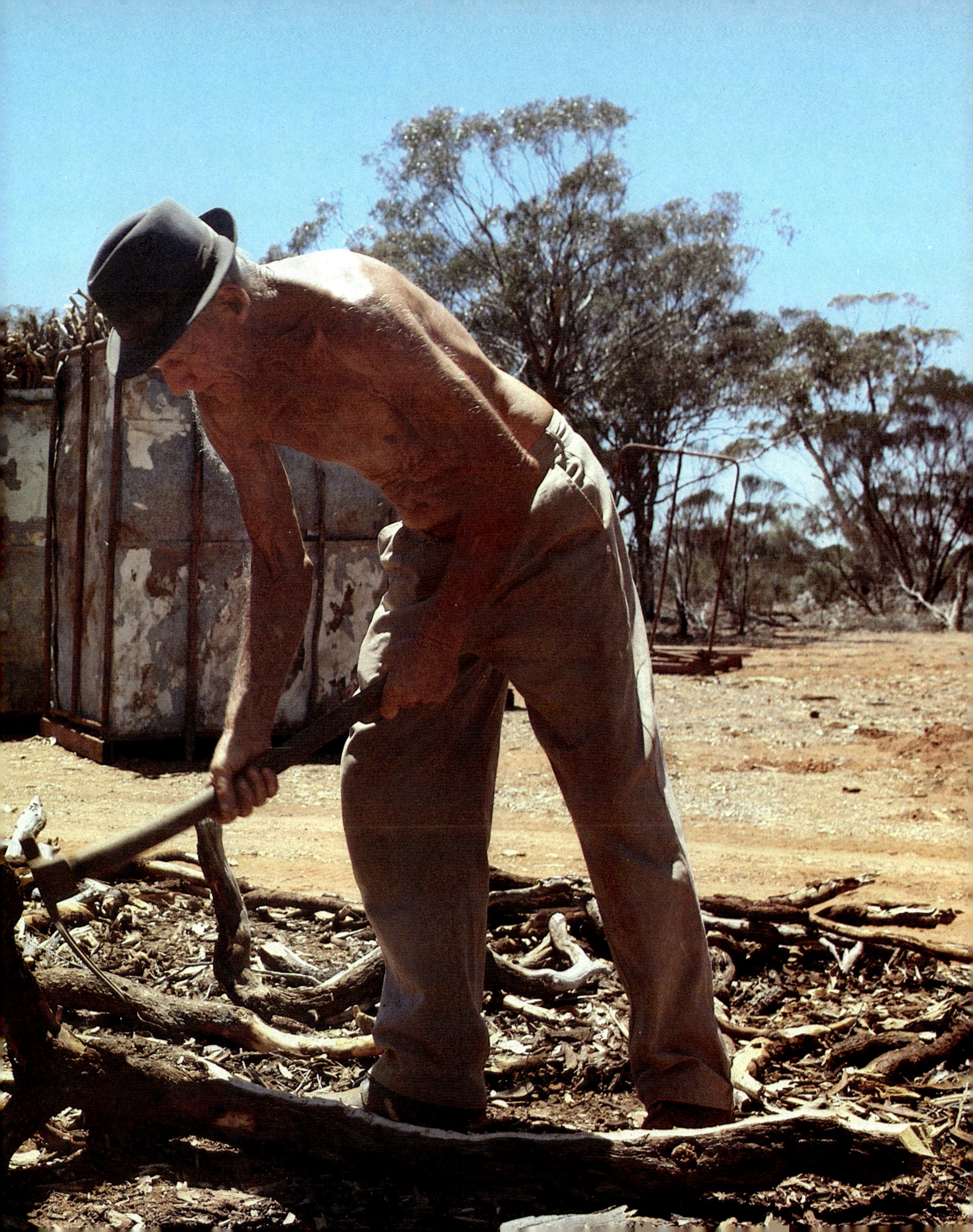

breakfast porridge, shaves and puts on his snap-brimmed felt hat (1950s vintage), and sets off for work.

He snigs the sandalwood roots out with a chain hitched to the back of his truck, then cleans them by hand, with an axe. He works seven hours a day, five and a half days a week, and once a week drives to Kalgoorlie to buy supplies, mainly grain from which he makes porridge and damper, and fruit. Bananas are the other staple of his diet.

Bill Savage owns a house in Kalgoorlie which he maintains as if it were a tent. He refuses to have electricity or water connected to it, and so he refuses to pay rate bills from the Kalgoorlie Council. He set out to establish total independence, eschewing the comforts and obligations of civilisation. In the past half-century only the Kalgoorlie Council's demands for rates (for services not used) have disturbed that dream. Bill's fight with the council is a small local *scandale*.

When he lived among men Bill Savage was a Communist. He still considers himself one, but these days marsupials and birds are his community. Kangaroos and parrots visit him daily to eat from his hand or drink from the water tins he leaves out for them. Such handouts would be unacceptable to him: his age entitles him to a pension but he will not take it; nor has he ever accepted the dole or any other social security benefit. 'I like work,' he said. He likes it and it is a matter of principle: the 8th article of the Communist Manifesto is 'Equal obligation to work'.

One of the last licensed sandalwood collectors left in the country, Bill Savage works seven hours a day, five and a half days a week, starting at 6 am. 'I like work,' he says. At eighty-three he is still fit and strong, a living advertisement for his outdoor life, a vegetarian diet, and no alcohol or tobacco.

THE WORKERS

DOWN THE MINES

Towards the end of the Tea and Sugar run, at Karoni, lived Fred Sullivan. At Karoni there were trees; there was water. Fred's wife had made a garden and kept chickens in her back yard. Her house was full of hanging plants. She was one of the women who had come to love this remote, quiet life. It was not, she said, as lonely as might be imagined. The Transcontinental line is an artery for all sorts of people — railway staff, mining engineers, ecologists, photographers. Whoever is travelling stops at most settlements en route, for a cup of tea and a chat; so in the course of a year the locals may well meet more new people than suburban city-dwellers do. Oliver was invited to a barbecue of sausages, and on Saturday afternoon he and the Sullivans went to Kalgoorlie for a game of swy.

Kalgoorlie is a gold and nickel town.

In 1893 one of the world's richest auriferous reefs, the Golden Mile, was discovered close to what is now Kalgoorlie.

The discovery of gold at Coolgardie in 1892, then Kalgoorlie a year later, was a godsend for Australia, for the 1890s was a period of frightful economic depression, drought and, in the eastern colonies, social and political turmoil. The supply of Victorian gold was diminishing. Once it had been so abundant that gold from Australia had made up forty per cent of the world's total annual gold production. With the discoveries at Coolgardie and Kalgoorlie, Western Australia became the new Golden Colony. Money was lavished on Kalgoorlie in wide roads and graceful buildings. Simply to establish the town was, in the paradigm of the time, 'to conquer' Nature. In 1903 water was pumped more than 5000 kilometres from the coast to the town. An English journalist, praising this enterprise, wrote that the pipeline to Kalgoorlie was 'the last great attack on Nature's defence of her treasure, and now she has capitulated'.

Despite advances in machinery and safety, coal mining is still dangerous and demanding. In the past, wooden stumps and beams were used to brace underground mines. Today metal bolts are inserted through special straps into the roof of the pit, ensuring much greater safety.

At coal mines in Newcastle, New South Wales, the lamp cabin is the check-in point where men collect their lights, batteries and self-rescuers (breathing apparatus) before going below.

R. JONES
GIBSON
164
166
167
168
169
170
G. ROSE
H. GRAY
T. EVANS
A. DICK
197
201
202
203

Jack Smythe, who labours at the John Darley mine in Newcastle, works on the longwall unit, a machine with cutting heads which moves back and forth along a coal face. Longwall mining is conducted on the retreat which means that once the machine is removed the roof and walls collapse.

Mining is male. Its imagery is violent and heroic: man tearing through the belly of a great, capricious female force. Geoffrey Blainey wrote: 'The underground miner battles a powerful and sometimes treacherous opponent. He is like a fisherman fighting the ocean'. But technological change softens this relationship.

The discovery of minerals in Australia has had a haphazard history, beginning with the discovery, by escaped convicts, of coal in New South Wales in 1791, and continuing with a series of splendid accidents. Until World War II mineral discoveries were the result of good eyesight, good luck and curiosity. It seemed as if Nature had to be caught off guard. But by the 1930s this sort of exploration was a tactical failure. Australia, according to these tactics, suffered insufficiencies in oil, copper, tin, aluminium, manganese, nickel, phosphate rock and sulphur. Since the war a range of exquisite tools for mineral exploration has become available: geochemistry, the electron probe micro-analyser, the atomic absorption spectrometer, aerial photography. Using these, Australia has enjoyed a truly spectacular success in discovering mineral deposits: nickel, manganese, copper, bauxite, minerals sands, natural gas, bismuth, uranium, lead-zinc, phosphate rock, oil, asbestos, antimony, tin and more and more and more iron ore and coal. By 1968 mining had replaced wool as Australia's major export industry. The imagery of taking by surprise and brute force seems inappropriate now; it may be more accurate to see miners — certainly those who find the deposits — as massaging the earth, not bludgeoning her.

Meanwhile, underground mining *is* perilous.

The only available demographic study of causes of death in various male occupations in Australia relates to data up to 1970. It found that mortality among miners, at 162 per cent, was the highest of any occupational group (i.e. everyone dies, so average mortality is 100 per cent at a certain age; some occupations have lower-

Most miners are relieved and exhausted at the end of their shift. In the gold mines of Kalgoorlie, the work is particularly stressful because of the continual danger and the high level of noise below the surface. At the same time as drilling is in operation, dump trucks and front-end loaders, weighing 20-30 tonnes, are constantly on the move.

than-average mortality, for example, farming.) But considering the extent and importance of the mining industry to Australia, disasters have been rare – and most, of course, have been associated with coal. The most serious accidents have been in New South Wales, in Victoria and Queensland: at Bulli on 23 March 1887, eighty-one miners were killed; at Mount Kembla on 31 July 1902 ninety-five men were killed in Australia's worst mine disaster. The horrors of dusting, the lung disease of coal miners, have now been overcome by improved safety measures and in Australia's coal mining towns one rarely sees the figures of ex-miners, blue-lipped on the hottest days, creeping, stopping to pant, and creeping again along the street. The air their sons and grandsons breathe down the mine is now filtered by masks, and all Australian miners wear hard-hats, protective boots, gloves and earmuffs – deafness being another occupational hazard for the miner.

Many safety measures have come into being as a result of pressure by the Australian Workers' Union, the association which covers most mining employees.

When Oliver visited a gold mine in Kalgoorlie at the end of his journey on the Tea and Sugar, the danger of underground mining was dramatically revealed to him. He, an AWU organiser known as Shakey, and a foreman went down into the Charlotte mine which had been blasted but not yet scaled. Scaling removes tons of rock, loosened by blasting and liable to fall off.

The foreman was in the lead, followed by Oliver, with Shakey bringing up the rear. Suddenly there was a tearing noise, rumbling and thunder, then screaming. Tons of rock had fallen from the walls of the mine, some of it crashing onto Shakey. The foreman was able to struggle back to the shaft to call for help while Oliver stayed beside the injured man. He recalled, 'We were alone there for probably only a few minutes but it seemed like days. Around us there was the noise of more landslides inside the mine, and the terrible groaning sound a person makes when his bones have been broken'.

The mine's emergency operations were excellent. In a few more minutes Shakey, lying now on a stretcher specially designed for mining accidents, had been hauled to the surface. An anxious crowd had gathered at the mine-head. Seeing their comrade in agony, bleeding, but obviously alive brought sighs and a gust of gallows wit. A miner shouted, 'Oh, Shakey – you'll do *anything* to get compo!'

Besides gold, Kalgoorlie is famous for girls: its Hay Street brothels of galvanised iron are on the itinerary of buses taking tourists around the famous sites and sights of the town. From time to time Press and pulpit have fulminated against Kalgoorlie's whorehouses. But according to local tradition it is the town's respectable women who have been just as determined as the miners that the brothels should stay, agreeing with the men that the prostitutes have a calming effect.

About once a month men from the concrete gang working on the Nullarbor go to Kalgoorlie for a night of drinking and paid sex, followed by a game of two-up next day.

Two-up or swy – probably from the German *zwei*, two – has been an Australian workers' game since the earliest days of the colonies, and is derived from the English pitch and toss. Its elements are few, and it seems to offer the gambler a chance. Two-up needs no fixtures or fittings and its implements fit or can hide in a man's pocket. Two-up is People's Gambling. In most parts of the country it is illegal, except on Anzac Day when, in memory of the diggers who loved it, it's played in every pub from Cairns to Broome. In opulent surroundings with croupiers in tuxedos some casinos now offer games of swy. The Kalgoorlie game is held in a round tin shed eight kilometres out of town. This casino has an earth

One of the few pleasures of miners at the Charlotte Gold Mine in Kalgoorlie is to take in the warmth of the morning sun, before going down below.

THE WORKERS 93

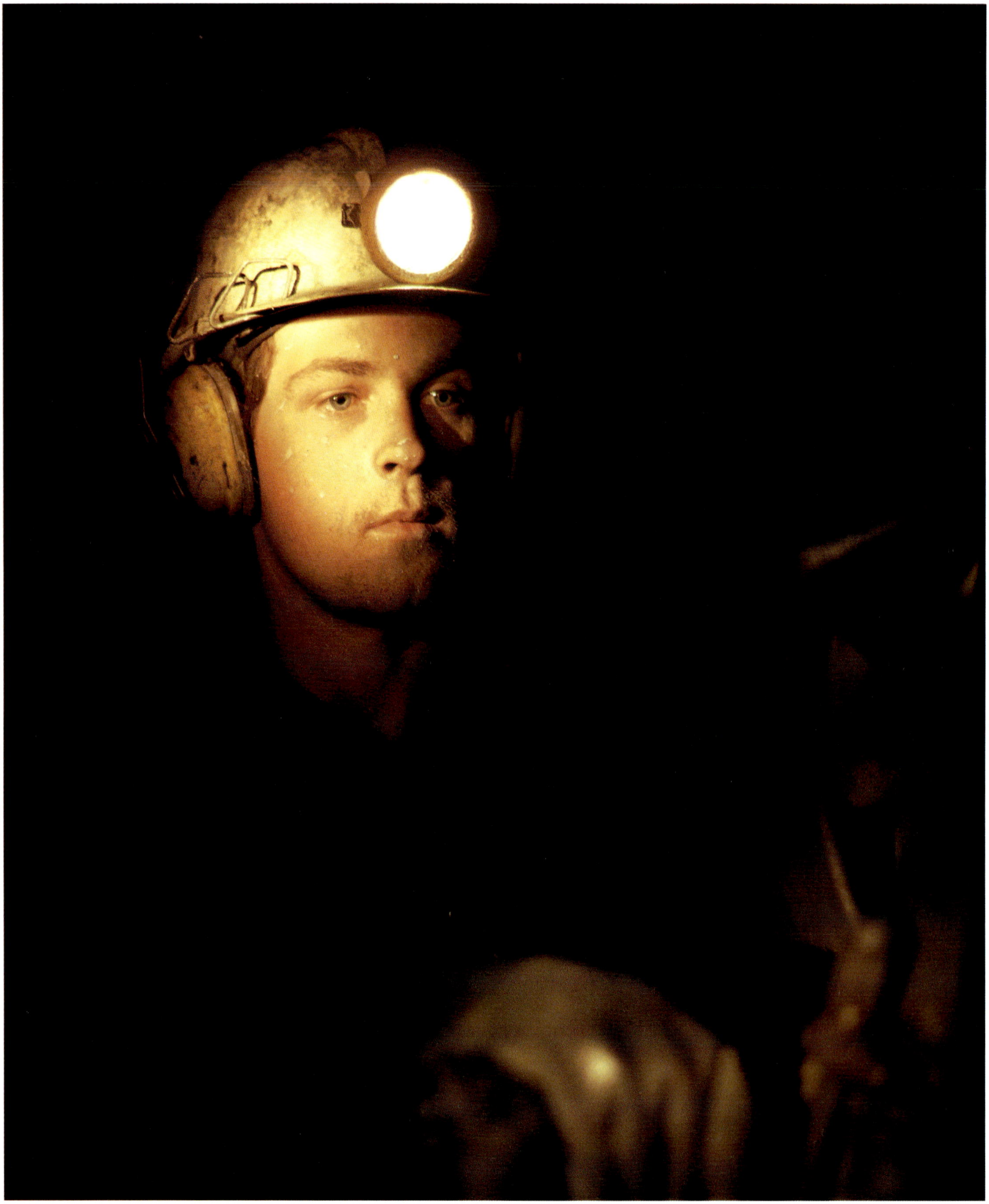

Although equipment and safety practices have vastly improved since the Mt Lyell copper mine in Tasmania was first opened last century (lights, helmets, steel boots, earmuffs and breathing apparatus have made conditions more tolerable) the life of a hardrock miner is still very tough.

Above It's a long day for coal miners in Newcastle. The 'set rider', Jimmy Marker, works the day shift on the drift transport (a kind of cable car) used to move equipment and men between the surface and the pit bottom, some 800 metres below the surface.

THE WORKERS 95

At the Mt. Lyall copper mine in Tasmania, workers assemble in front of the 'Main Decline', the single entrance to the entire underground complex, prior to starting their shift. Safety regulations and 'crib times' (the miners' meal and tea breaks) are posted on large signs at the entrance. Unlike smoke-ohs and meal breaks where the worker can move away from his workplace, miners cannot escape the pit.

DECLINE 1973

PRINCE LYELL MINE
GO FOR SAFETY
STOP ACCIDENTS
DAYS SINCE LAST L.T.A.

HAVE YOU
1. CHECKED ENTRANCE TO PLACE OF WORK
2. CHECKED WORKPLACE AND EQUIPMENT ARE IN GOOD ORDER
3. CHECKED MEN ARE WORKING PROPERLY
4. DONE AN ACT OF SAFETY
5. ENSURED THAT YOUR MEN CAN AND WILL CONTINUE TO WORK PROPERLY

PRINCE LYELL
CRIB TIMES
ALL EMPLOYEES

FIRING TIMES
ALL AREAS

DO NOT ENTER
DECLINE
IF BLUE LIGHT IS
FLASHING

floor and is open to the sky, apart from a bit of roofing around the sides. There are a few wooden benches for the players to sit on; the other amenity is a nearby 10,000 gallon water tank, cut in half to make 'Ladies' and 'Men's' lavatories. There were about twenty players, mostly white men, an Aborigine, and a Chinese woman clutching a fistful of $50 bills. Fred Sullivan was chosen to be Spinner for a game.

The rite of swy is that players bet on whether two pennies, held in a wooden kip, when tossed in the air by the spinner, will come down heads or tails. If the coins fall as odds – one heads, one tails – all bets are frozen. The coins must rise at least one metre above the spinner's head, they must spin, and they are not permitted to touch in the air. If the spinner can throw three pairs of heads without throwing tails, or five odds in a row, he picks up 15/2 on his wager. The game is judged by a Boxer, traditionally a man capable of thumping players or spinners who get out of hand. The Boxer calls the ritual instruction to throw – three words which have been uttered in every Australian army camp from New Guinea to Palestine: 'Come in, Spinner!'

Left Two-up, people's gambling, is an Australian institution. Players bet on whether two pennies, held in a wooden kip, when tossed in the air by the 'spinner', will come down heads or tails. In most parts of Australia two-up is illegal. This game is being played eight kilometres from Kalgoorlie, the famous gold-mining town in Western Australia.

Above The traditional end to the Australian working day. In the isolated gulf country of north-western Queensland Glen Morgan and Mark Allen enjoy a cold beer in the back bar of the National Hotel, Normanton – known locally as the 'Purple Pub'. For Glen and Mark this is their first trip to town in three months.

THE WORKERS 99

IN THE SHEDS

The Australian Workers' Union began as a shearers' union, in Ballarat, in 1886. Its first president was the saintly William Spence. For Spence, as for many others then and since, trade unionism was an expression of Christian ethics and spirituality.

The age of faith was on its last legs by the end of the nineteenth century. In 1882 Nietzsche had dared to write what people feared: 'The greatest modern event – that God is dead... is beginning to cast its first shadow across Europe.' That shadow had been felt for years in the Australian bush: either God was dead, or he was not a loving God but one hostile to man, and life seemed comfortless and without meaning.

> We have come 16,000 miles to better our condition, and not to act as a mere part of machinery; and it is neither right nor just that we should cross the trackless regions of immensity between us and our fatherland, to be rewarded with excessive toil, a bare existance, and a premature grave. – James Galloway, a pioneer of the Eight Hours' Movement.

The trade union movement filled that part of the human heart which demands to reach beyond the individual and bring him and her into contact with existence on deeper and broader levels. Spence wrote: 'Unionism came to the Australian bushman as a religion. It came bringing salvation from years of tyranny. It had in it that feeling of mateship which he understands already... Membership of the union makes a man a better husband, a better father and a better and more active citizen.'

There had been plenty of tyranny in the shearing game. The first shearers were convicts. Unlike slaves in the American colonies, it was not necessary to buy convicts – the Crown handed them out, gratis, to subjects with whom it was

There are always small scraps of wool left over after the fleece is shorn. Stained pieces, belly wools and locks are each collected in separate baskets, later to be baled.

According to Henry Lawson, 'the shearer on the board... is a demon'. At Nine Mile Station, outside Broken Hill, shearers do an average of 100-120 sheep a day. Since the introduction of wide combs the shearer's daily tally has increased, while the board-boy's (shedhand) work has become much harder for the same day's pay. Nine Mile, a 20,000 hectare run with a five-stand shed (each shearer's cubicle is known as a stand), boasts about 8000 sheep.

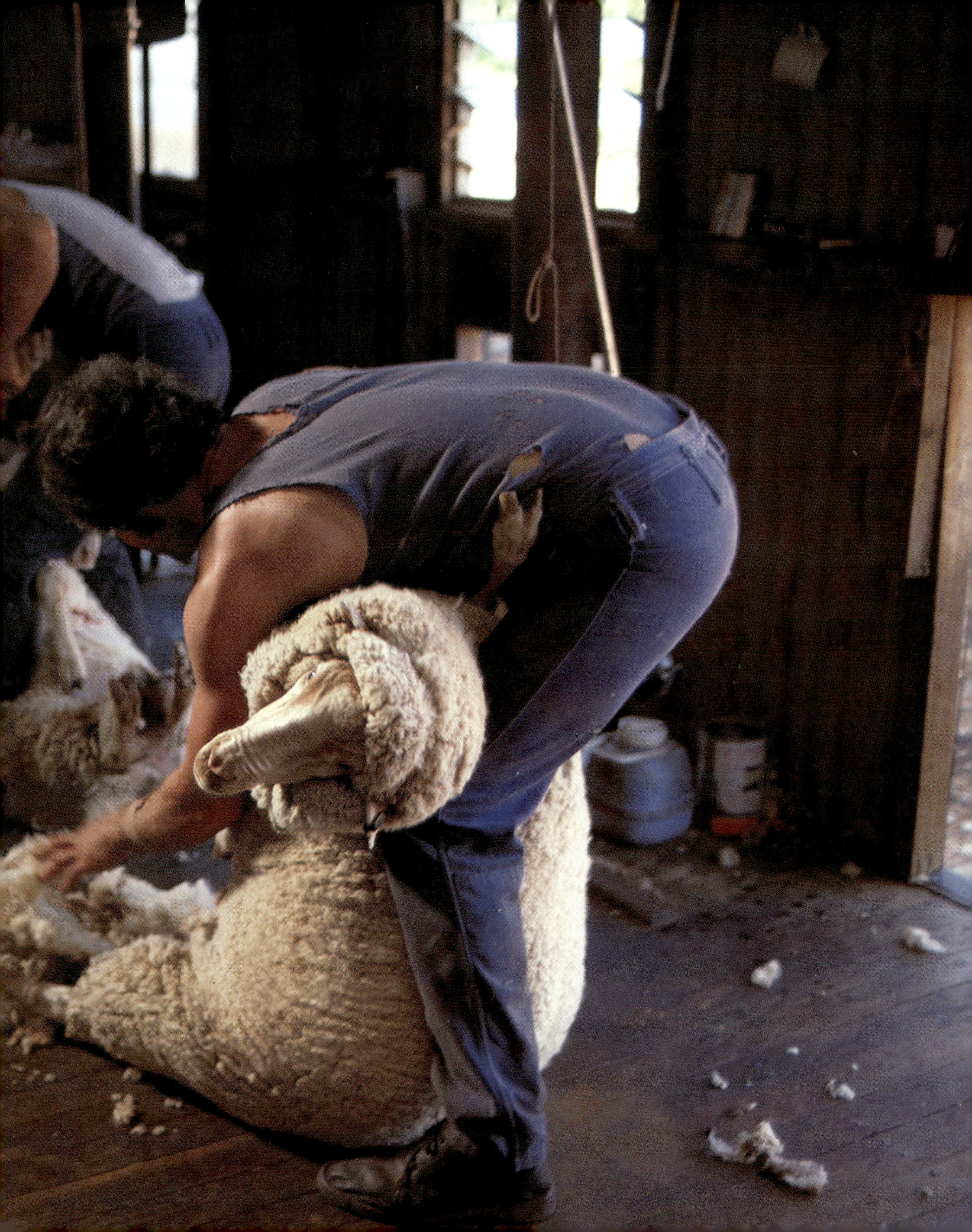

pleased. There was, therefore, no economic incentive to look after them properly or treat them better than beasts. It was convicts who, in 1822, began a proto-trade union movement in Australia when they attempted to organise for better rations and higher nominal rates of pay. They were beaten and their leader was put to the lash. Legislation had been passed in England making unionism illegal in the colonies; it was only in 1825 that the Act was repealed and unionism decriminalised. Establishing a union for shearers in the Australian colonies was daunting and much more difficult than establishing unions for city workers. In the country there were vast distances to overcome, lack of transport, lack of a communication technology, nomadic lifestyle, and a lack of men with the extra energy to appoint themselves leaders of such an undertaking. There was also hostility from the squatters. A woolgrower friendly to the idea of shearers combining to improve their conditions was Simon Fraser, grandfather to the former Prime Minister, Malcolm Fraser, on whose property, Nyang in the New South Wales Riverina district, the germ of the shearers' union took root, in 1886.

The formation of the shearing union was straw in a wind that, within a few years, was a storm. From 1888 to 1902 shearers' strikes raged across Queensland and New South Wales. The Riot Act was read in Wagga Wagga. A woolgrower wrote to the *Brisbane Courier*: 'I honestly think that if a little blood were shed a great deal of good would result.' He was not thinking, apparently, of his own blood. The letter inspired Henry Lawson to reply:

> We'll make the tyrant feel the sting
> O' those that they would throttle
> They needn't say the fault is ours,
> If blood should stain the wattle.

The shearers, who in Queensland had organised themselves as a para-military force, were defeated. From this defeat came the birth of the Labor Party, and also an association of pastoralists who later formed into the Country (now the National) Party. Australia was on the edge of its first great depression.

The emotional tone of the AWU owes much to the traumas surrounding its most tender years. A shearers' ditty of those days runs:

> May the Lord above send down a dove
> With wings as sharp as razors
> To cut the throats of bloody scabs
> Who cut down poor men's wages.

The hatred of scabs — scab being a sheep disease — was given unbridled verbal expression. An ode to a scab runs:

> And when I hear you're buggered
> And your life they will not save
> I'll slip across the border
> And piss upon your grave.

Others are too obscene to quote.

A dye had been cast. Ninety years later, during the wide-comb dispute, the AWU reacted with a protectiveness for 'us' and an animosity towards 'them' — 'New Zealand mongrels' — which seemed extreme to outsiders.

Shearers, being itinerants, have a tradition of adventure and living rough. They have always travelled in groups — on foot, horseback, camel, bicycle, train, and, these days, by car. They camped and lived off the land in between 'runs' and until the late nineteenth century began work at 6 am and worked until dusk five days a week, on Saturdays until 4 pm. Their huts were crude: unlined galvanised iron with two tiers of bunks and chaff bags filled with dry grass or whatever was handy. In a

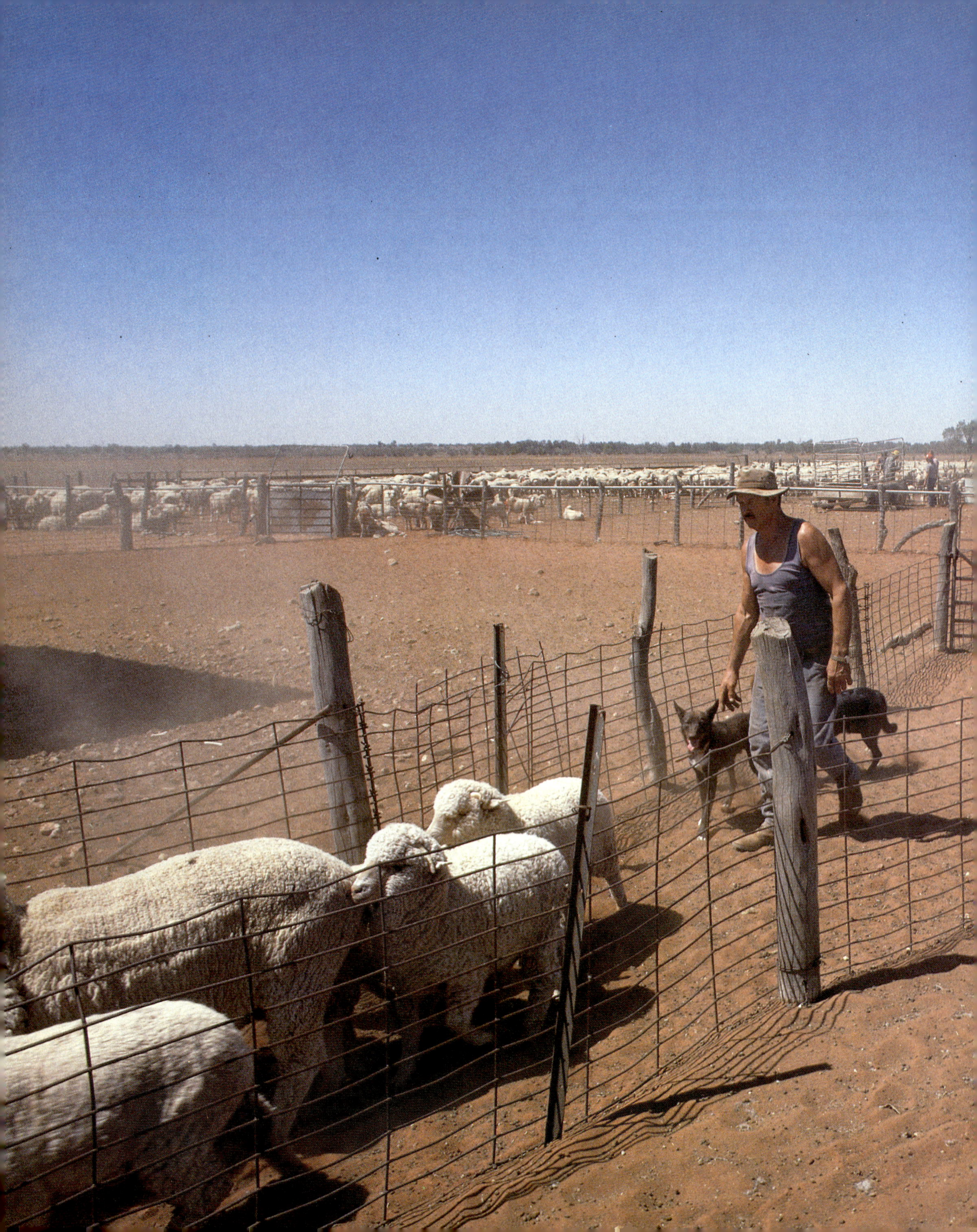

A stationhand herds in the sheep for shearing at Tongo Station, a 28,000 hectare sheep-run in the red-soil country of north-western New South Wales.

press interview, the secretary of the Lightning Ridge branch of the AWU, Don Johnson, recalled the hardships of this century: 'When I started shearing back in '45, they'd give you a hessian bag to sleep on and you'd fill it with straw, which was full of thistles, dogshit, fleas and Christ knows what. There was no refrigeration at all and the cockies made it a crime to take a drink on to the place. The handpiece you'd shear with would get so hot you could fry an egg on it.'

The earliest Australian shearers held the sheep on their laps and clipped at them with a pair of scissors. Sheep had been shorn like this since Biblical days. By the end of the nineteenth century the distinctive, new Australian skill, handshearing, with the sheep sitting on its backside, was an artform.

The maestro was Jack Howe, who had hands 'like small tennis rackets' and who could shear more than 300 sheep in one day, with handshears. He was a celebrity and he made all shearers glamorous. The combination of dogged commitment to a cause and physical prowess has made the shearer the archetype of the Australian working man. He is the civilian Anzac, a figure surrounded with symbols and symbolic acts.

One of them is humorous talk. Shearers are – or should be – laconic wits. Paul Hogan should have been a shearer; Mick Young, a minister in the Hawke government, was a shearer and his light, sharp, agile tongue made him one of the most popular men in parliament. Patsy Adam-Smith quotes some mind-boggling examples of shearing talk:

'The bait-slinger chiakked the blue-tongue but that brownie-gorger called for some roll-me-in-the-gutter for his dodger and sand for his burgoo – and the babbler headed for the mulga saying he'd not cook for a sword swallower.' This, in English, means: The shearers' cook rebuked the greedy shearer, but he (that lover of sweet brown-sugar currant loaf)

Part of the job of the contractor is to 'count out' the sheep. It's a very skilled job involving a quick eye, good arithmetic and lots of experience. As the shorn sheep spring out from their crowded, dusty pen, the contractor has to count them. He keeps a record in his 'tallybook' of how many each shearer has shorn. At Tongo Station, which has an eight-stand shed, the contractor has to keep track of no less than 15,000 sheep during shearing time.

Dinner for shearers is in the middle of the day and usually consists of meat and vegetables. At Kentucky Station, in the New England region of New South Wales, it comes after the second shift (or 'run') at noon. By then each shearer will have been on the board for four hours, having shorn fifty or sixty sheep. There are normally four runs: 7.30-9.30, 10.00-12.00, 1.00-3.00 and 3.30-5.30.

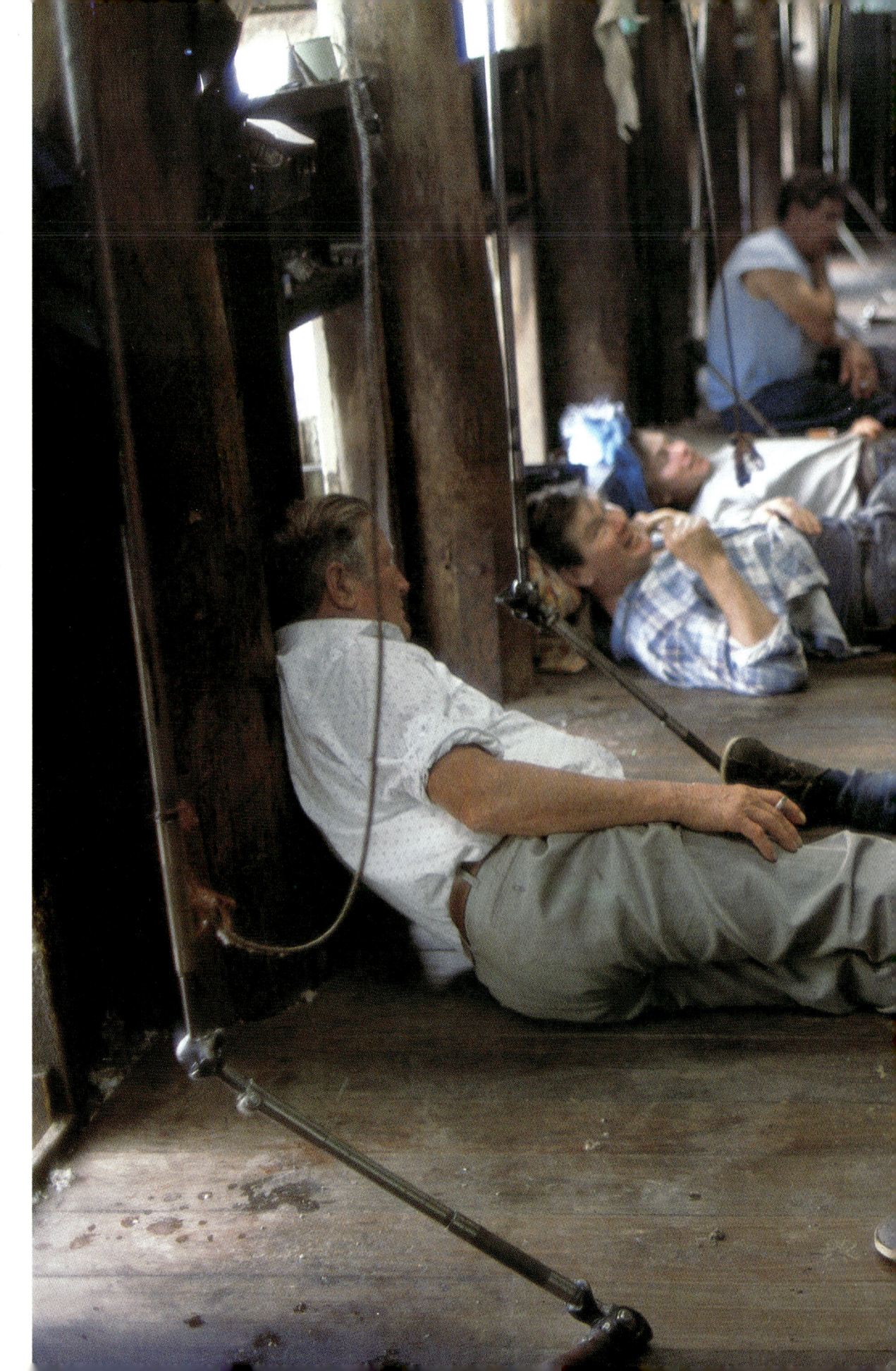

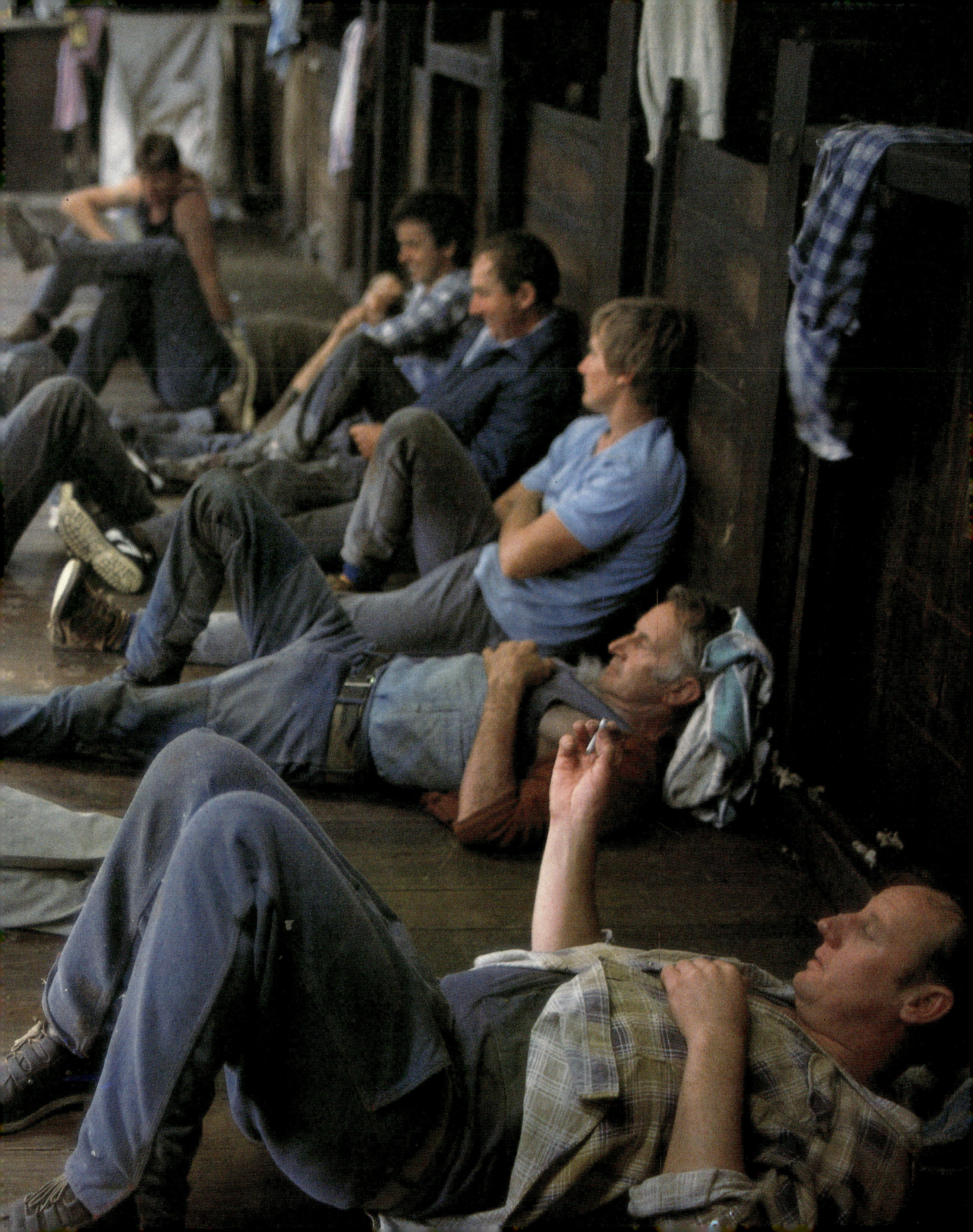

An organiser with the Australian Workers' Union for twenty-six years, Bluey Rodwell has the toughness, yet kindness which goes with someone who understands what it's like to work hard. 'You've got to have a pretty big heart for this work', he said after being confronted by angry shearers during the wide-comb dispute.

called for butter for his bread and sugar for his porridge. At which the cook left, saying he'd not cook for a man who ate off his knife.

A contractor remarked of a female cook he had hired that she was so tough she 'could eat an apple through the dog fence'.

Shearers' male cooks are notorious drunks and prima donnas, but then shearers are notoriously hard to please about food. There have been cooks with names such as Tasteless George, who could remove the taste from bacon; the Holy Ghost, who resurrected yesterday's dishes, and 1080, the name of a weed killer. There was also Old Maggotty, whose meat walked off the serving dish, they said.

The strain of shearing makes good, easily digested food, essential. Shearers stand bent over for most of the day, cramping the digestive tract and straining the back and central nervous system. Quick-ese, the indigestion tablet, is called 'the shearer's lolly'. There are men still shearing at seventy, but according to Bluey Rodwell of the AWU, 'Most shearers are knocked up by the age of fifty'. When Oliver accompanied Bluey into shearing sheds he noticed how often a man, straightening up between sheep, would have to uncramp his back by pushing a fist into his spine. Yoga and the Alexander Technique have a lot to offer shearers.

In 1984-85 shearers cut the wool from 166.8 million sheep and lambs, with an average fleece weight of 4.43 kilograms. Five years earlier Australian fleeces weighed on average 4.33 kilograms. The 1984-85 wool clip, exported, earned $2.4 billion, which was 15.1 per cent of the value of total agricultural production, exported. During the Korean War boom, wool exports earned 55.6 per cent of all agricultural industries.

Each year, after the AWU convention in January, union organisers set out for country districts for the ritual of 'selling The Ticket'. The Ticket is the AWU

Smoke-oh for some station hands means having a break from ear marking and the gruesome task of cutting and docking (cutting off the sheep's testicles and tails). Even more bloody is mulesing which involves using shears to cut the skin off around the sheep's anus. It eventually heals into scar tissue and so prevents the sheep becoming flyblown.

membership, costing $115 in 1987. Selling it and buying it is a tribal rite, symbolising solidarity among shearers and between them and the guardian of their livelihood, that totem, the union.

Oliver travelled with two organisers, Mick O'Shea and Bluey Rodwell. Bluey has been selling the ticket for almost a quarter of a century. He is a big, shrewd, devout unionist who refers to those who introduced the wide-comb as 'wife-starving mongrels' and 'bash artists'. (There has been plenty of bash artistry on both sides of the wide-comb dispute.) Bluey doesn't need to raise his voice when making such remarks: he has a presence which suggests authority. In a troubled, dispute-torn industry, as shearing has been for the past four years, a union organiser needs to be both parish priest and arm-twister. He comes as a shoulder for members to cry on, with a big fist at the end of it. Oliver said, 'I was struck by how patient Bluey was. The number of complaints a union organiser must listen to is astonishing. Of course the shearers have nobody else to complain to about their lives, so when the organiser turns up he has to listen to all their problems: machinery that doesn't work, dirty accommodation, the union letting him down, a run-in with a woolgrower... Bluey would listen to all these complaints. He'd be dead tired by seven o'clock at night.'

Bluey said, 'I like to have a few Red Mill rums at the end of the day'.

The tickets are sold from February to the end of July. Bluey begins in the north of the West Darling area, staying in motels where he can, camping out otherwise, arranging his accommodation so that he will be able to arrive at his first shed for the day at morning smoke-oh, 9.30. He travels at least 300 kilometres a day. For the past few years, while the wide-comb dispute has been raging, AWU organisers have travelled in twos – like policemen patrolling the East End of London – because of the threat of violence. When the union organiser arrives a shed can explode.

Bluey explained: 'There'll be a cocky's son in there shearing, a young would-be capitalist who doesn't want to buy a ticket, or one of those anti-union blokes. And the men will refuse to go on working until he joins up. Sometimes the members get so irate they won't let these characters join – won't let me sell them a ticket. There are shouts of 'Get out of the shed', and they hunt those mongrels off the place.'

On other occasions in the past few years Bluey has turned up at sheds and been met with silence and stony eyes. He has had all his tyres let down. 'You've got to have a pretty big heart for this work,' he said. Although he was never a shearer he seems personally affronted by the introduction of the wide-comb: 'The Australian shearers were the greatest tradesmen in the world with the narrow comb. But with this wide comb, it's pathetic. It can knock the wool off all right, but there's less skill and quality: it's a lawn mower. Where there used to be one bale of locks, there are now three. There are more second cuts and there's more wool going back to the paddock. You can't get up the neck of a big merino with one of those contraptions. A lot of the smaller graziers are already asking for a return to the narrow comb.'

From the outset the AWU leadership treated the wide-comb dispute as an argument about values – is it moral? – and not about facts – is it efficient? The narrow comb was made to symbolise Truth, Beauty and the True Shearer, the Archetypal Mate. The wide-comb was described by AWU officials as 'immoral and repulsive'. It was Satan's thing. But it shears sheep fast and it is now universally used in Australia: the union was forced to abandon its emotional, value-laden opposition in the face of a revolt by shearers. One aspect of this messy dispute is that wide-combers, charged with immorality, have tended to flout the shearers' award whenever it suits them. 'They work all sorts of hours – Saturdays, Sundays – until they knock up,' Bluey said. Shearers' conditions of work have been hard won; before unionisation the woolgrower set the rules and was the sole judge of them. There were pastoralists who boasted of cheating shearers out of their pay. The

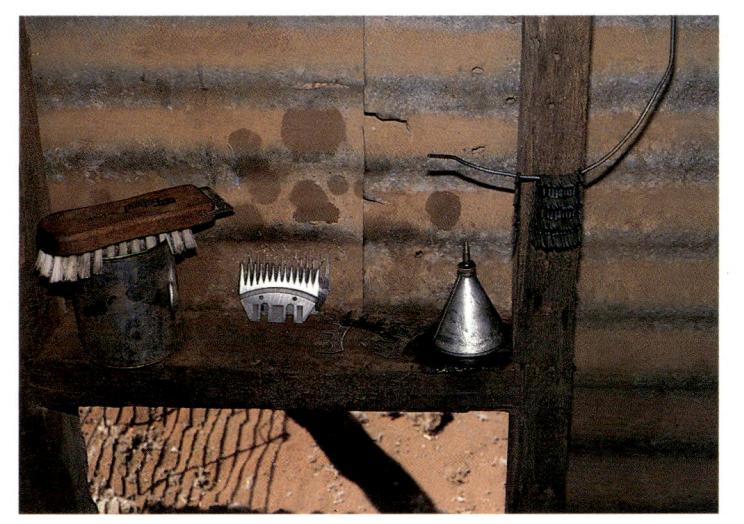

Left The shearer's tool kit has remained the same for years: a tin bucket, a brush, an oil can, screwdriver, needle and thread, comb and cutters – in this instance, a wide comb.

Above Smoke-oh at Kentucky Station is no time to relax. Shearers have to clean and oil their comb and cutters used in the previous run, and reload the hand piece. And the 'expert', or 'contractor', who organises a team of shearers and makes the agreements with the property owner, is likely to be sharpening and grinding the comb and cutters as well. Kentucky Station is one of the few places where the narrow comb was still used until quite recent times.

THE WORKERS 117

strikers of the 1890s and of 1956 – the last shearing strike before the wide-comb dispute – held out until they and their families half-starved. With such a history behind their industrial award, it's not surprising that those who breach it are considered much worse than harlots – they are traitors.

The shearing photographs in these pages were taken on a ticket selling excursion which began in Wilcannia and fanned out to stations with names like Tongo, Perry, Murtee, Polpah, Myall, Kalkaroo and Yantabangee. Oliver recalled, 'We'd be going along in Bluey's panel van, which has a mattress, cooking utensils and a water bottle in the back. Bluey would be neatly dressed: hair combed flat, ironed shirt, shiny shoes – he was very conscious of being properly turned out for work each day. We'd be chatting and somehow he'd turn the conversation to, say, kangaroos. 'I know every kangaroo round here and I've signed most of them up,' he'd say. And then a few minutes later he'd add, 'Oh, there are a few of my members' – and there would be a family of kangaroos ahead of us. He had superb eyesight and he'd seen them a couple of minutes earlier, but he'd kept it up his sleeve as a surprise. He's playful, in that laconic way. It seemed to be important to selling the ticket. He would walk into a shed and say, "I've got a few lottery tickets..."'

Shearers receive no superannuation, long service or sick leave, or holiday pay. Whether male or female – there are some female shearers – they earn $109 per hundred sheep and get about eight months' work a year from shearing, if willing to travel. For the rest of the year they find what work they can. According to Bluey Rodwell, 'Maybe a bit of crutching, or wheat lumping'.

At Kentucky Station, where 20,000 sheep are shorn annually, the 'tussock jumper' (station hand) rounds up the sheep on his motor bike, with the help of his dog.

WHEAT, COTTON AND CANE

Wheat is grown in the same areas as wool, in all states except the Northern Territory. In 1984-85 wheat and wheaten flour exports earned $2.8 billion, more than a third of the value of all our agricultural exports. The Middle East, the USSR and China are customers for Australian wheat which, like most other successful agricultural industries in this country owes its success to artifice. It was the agricultural scientist William Farrer who, in 1885 and 1898 experimented successfully in breeding rust-resistant wheat, and wheat which could be grown in dry areas.

Since the 1960s cotton has been grown alongside of, or in place of wheat in some areas in New South Wales and Queensland. Since 1970 the land put to cotton has increased dramatically, for it became obvious that the market for cotton was lucrative and safe. More than three-quarters of Australia's total production of cotton is grown in New South Wales, principally in the Namoi, Macquarie, Gwydir and McIntyre Valleys, and the Bourke area. Almost the whole crop — ninety-two per cent — is exported, to markets in East and South-East Asia which seem able to use all the cotton we can supply. In 1979-80 the value of raw cotton exported was $66.9 million; in 1985-86 this had leapt to $259.6 million.

American companies first planted cotton in Australia, in the Wee Waa area, and set out to follow the American practice of using non-union labour. The AWU waged a long struggle to organise the cotton chippers — the people who weed the cotton 'blocks' — which was won, in 1965, when female chippers in the Macquarie Valley decided to join the union. Before then there had been cases of 'spontaneous combustion' in bins of cotton belonging to growers who refused to entertain the idea of unionised workers. Ironically, for the growers, their industry has benefited from unionisation, for it now has a reliable (largely female) workforce.

Bluey Rodwell was responsible for signing up many of the cotton chippers and takes pride in having established a local workforce of 300 people in the Macquarie

The grain bunker, essentially a huge woven-polyester tarpaulin, like this one at Werris Creek near Tamworth, New South Wales, holds some 40,000 tonnes of wheat. Bunker storage is an ancient method dating back to the Pharoahs; a technology which Australia has developed and refined, and now exports to Middle-East countries and the United States.

THE WORKERS 121

But for the Burrendong Dam, the cotton fields in the north-west of New South Wales would not exist. Nor would there be work for the women who come from the nearby towns of Narromine, Trangie, Warren and Gilgandra. Known as cotton chippers, these women use a hoe to weed row after row of cotton before it is picked. It is back-breaking work which has to be carried out in the hottest season.

Valley. 'If I had my way all the chippers would be women,' he said. 'They're great workers. When the plants are little the women really care for them. The blokes are off looking under a tree.' As the cotton grows taller men are often needed to chip the very large weeds which infest the fields, so at least until the day when chipping, too, is mechanised, it will remain a mixed-gender job.

Chippers work two rows of cotton at a time, using a hoe to chip to the left and right of them as they walk along fields which stretch to the horizon and beyond. Cotton fields in New South Wales are so exquisitely graded that a track a kilometre long falls just a few centimetres, just enough for water to trickle through its web of irrigation canals. The chippers begin soon after sunrise so that they can work six to seven hours and be finished by 1 pm when the intense heat of these great sculpted plains makes further labour impossible. They eat lunch around 10 am in a mobile dining room, a truck fitted out with a table and benches, with a roof for shade and cyclone wire sides. Some chippers sit underneath the truck, where it's cooler. The dining truck is part of their industrial award, won by the AWU, as is a second amenity: the Porta-Loo. There is one for the men, another for the women. Cotton chippers earn $7.80 an hour and have no penalty rates. They get work chipping from November to April. If they are itinerants, they may then go on to picking autumn fruit and winter vegetables, or may go north for the sugarcane harvest, from June to December.

Australia may, however, be regarded as the
paradise of working men, when they choose to avail themselves of
the advantages which it offers. Here there is always plenty of
profitable work for the industrious. – Samuel Smiles, *A Boy's
Voyage Around The World.*

Pesticides are used at many stages in the course of growing cotton. Just before harvesting the crop is sprayed with a defoliant which makes the field easier to harvest and gives a better quality cotton.

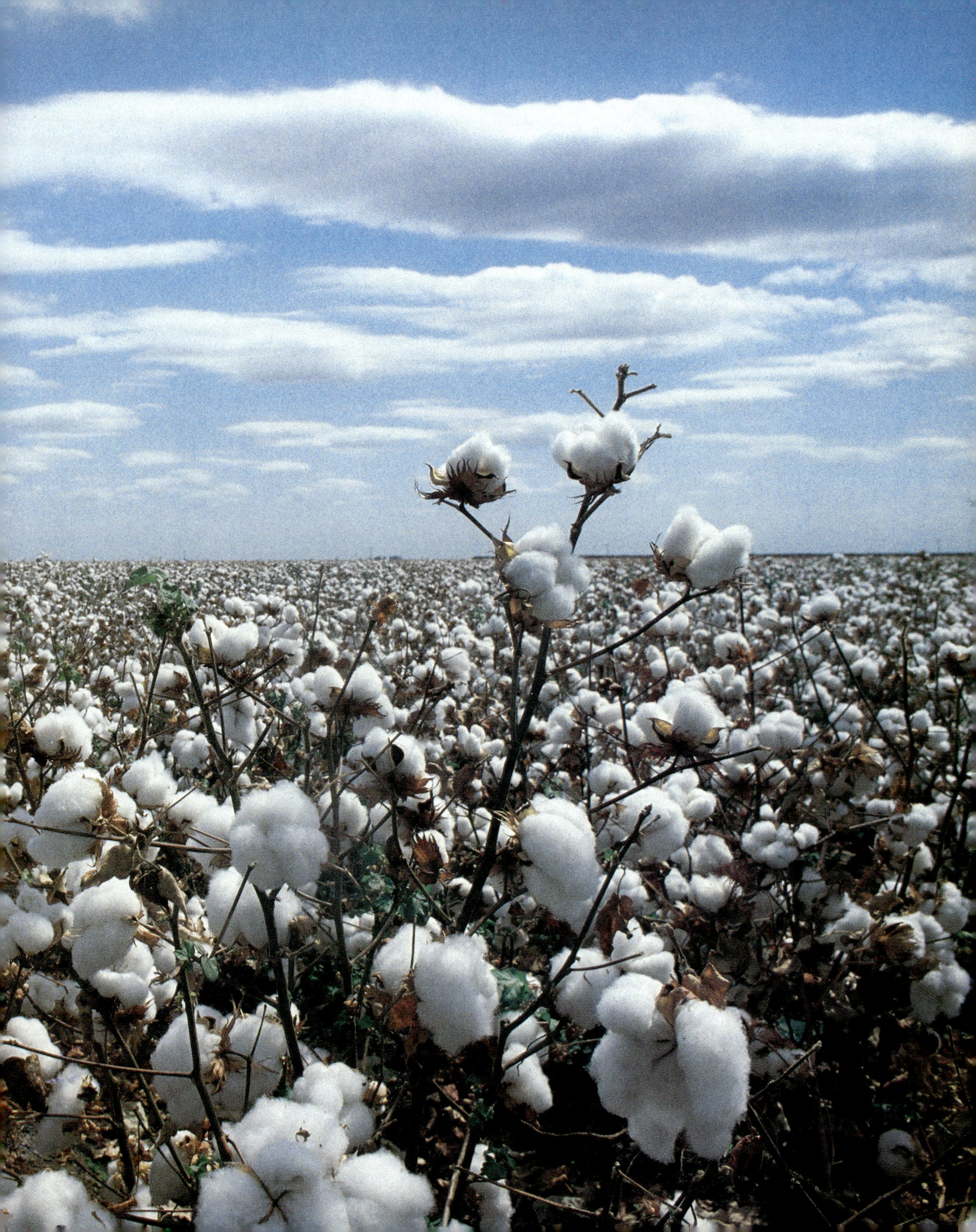

Cotton chippers work hard, but there's still time for romance. The woman on the left proudly displays her newly acquired engagement ring.

Australian cane farmers are regarded as among the most efficient in the world. They were the first in the world to introduce mechanical cultivation and harvesting techniques, and by 1964 the entire industry had converted to bulk handling. Ploughing, planting, harvesting and transportation of sugarcane is all done mechanically, so cane farming is much easier than it used to be, but it's still a hot, grimy way to earn a living. In the West Indian colonies cane cutters were slaves, and after slavery was abolished, indentured labour from India was imported to cut cane. In Australia we imported South Sea Islanders, 'Kanakas', to work the cane fields – as if cane cutting were too intense a job for white men. There is one shot of a man who looks almost demonic, a real earth-spirit or chthonic apparition, as he stands before his field of flames.

So intense is the heat of burning cane that farmers consider it safer to light their fields just on sunset when the day has cooled down. With wet sacks close to hand, the men watch for 'floaters' (burning leaves) which drift upwards with the heat and can start secondary fires.

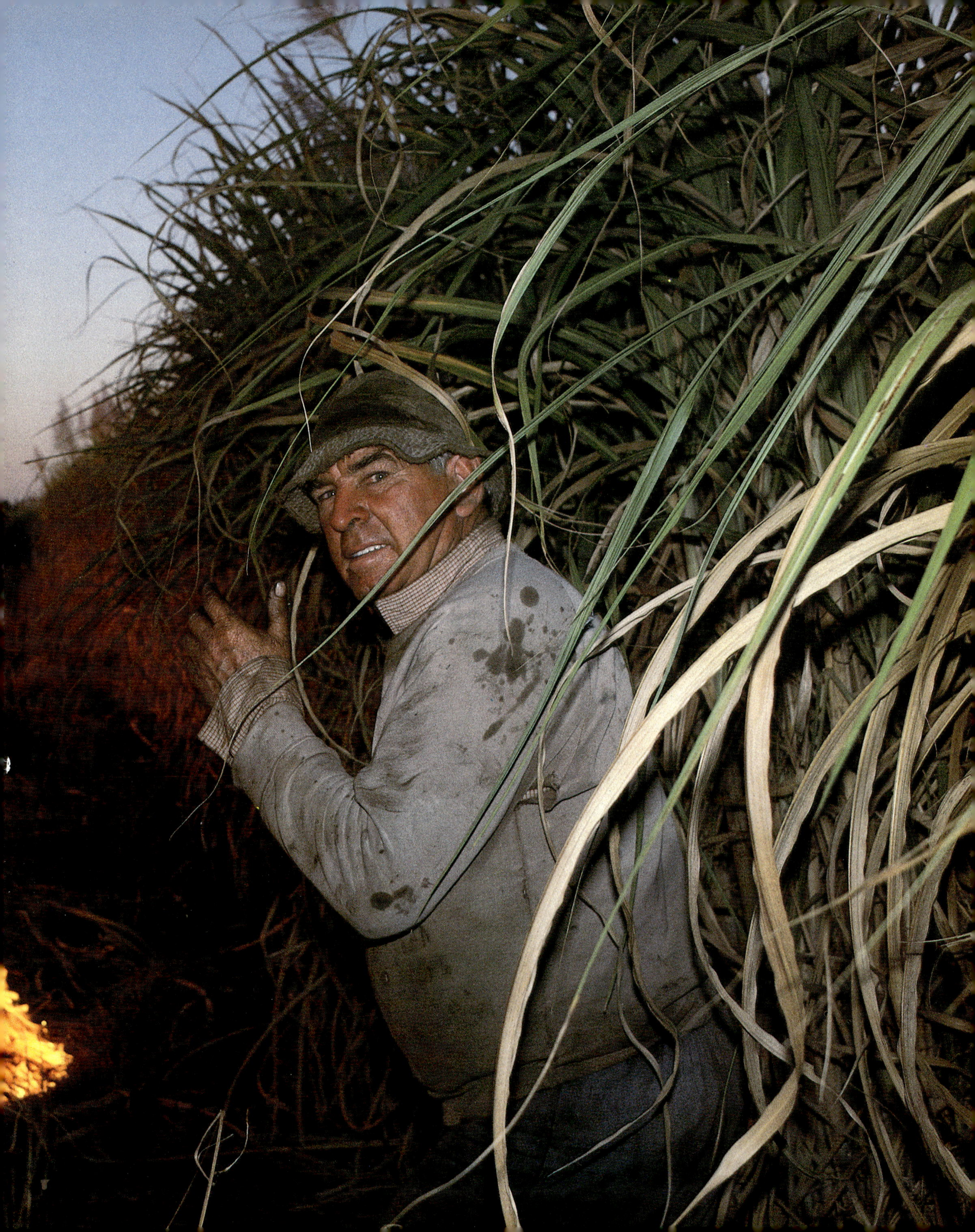

The 'fire bug', which is being blown out by this boy in the cane fields near Nambour in Queensland, is used to set alight the sugar cane prior to harvest. This ingenious device consists of a long rigid metal hose fed by a reservoir of kerosene at one end. The flow of the kerosene is regulated by a small trigger to leave the required trail of flames along the edge of the field. 'Burning' makes harvesting easier. It also gets rid of the snakes.

During harvest time the sugar cane train runs almost continuously through the main street of Nambour and across the Bruce Highway (Queensland's main north-south highway) often holding up traffic.

THE WORKERS 131

ITINERANTS

Each year until the 1960s an army of men and women moved from the cane fields north of the Tropic of Capricorn, down through New South Wales to the Victorian Riverina, and back again. They often travelled in families, the children working alongside their parents. They picked spuds in Dorrigo, pears in Shepparton, then moved into Mildura in the Murray Irrigation area for the orange season. The children attended school irregularly or not at all. Their parents were often illiterate and they would probably be, too. Their lives were free and hard, and it was these nomads who made it possible to transform huge tracts of bush into farmland in a few generations. Without the itinerants it would have been impossible, in such sparsely populated country, for the harvest in wool and wheat and fruit and vegetables to be gathered.

Year by year there are fewer of them. Until recently the pickers were unionised only here and there, but that too is changing. The AWU wants to help the fruit and vegetable pickers and will be able to do so through industrial pressure on their employers, the growers, who are now exporting more and more produce. This is good and bad news for the itinerants. It means that they finally have protection from unfair employment practices, but it also means they lose the freedom which has been theirs for generations.

Already more than a quarter of Australia's fruit is exported; fruit and vegetables exports in 1984-85 earned $260 million, of which $58 million was from vegetables, and year by year the industry increases its yields, due to breeding, irrigation and better control of disease and insect pests. On half the amount of land used for growing vegetables in 1945, there was double the yield of crops by 1975. The increasing efficiency of Australian potato growing, for example, is shown by recent statistics: in 1979-80, 857 tonnes of potatoes were grown; five years later, on the same area, more than one million tonnes were grown.

Pear picking near Shepparton, in the Goulburn Valley region of Victoria, attracts both professional pickers, who return each season, and casual workers. This picker has worked in the region for many years. Most of the pears are bound for the cannery.

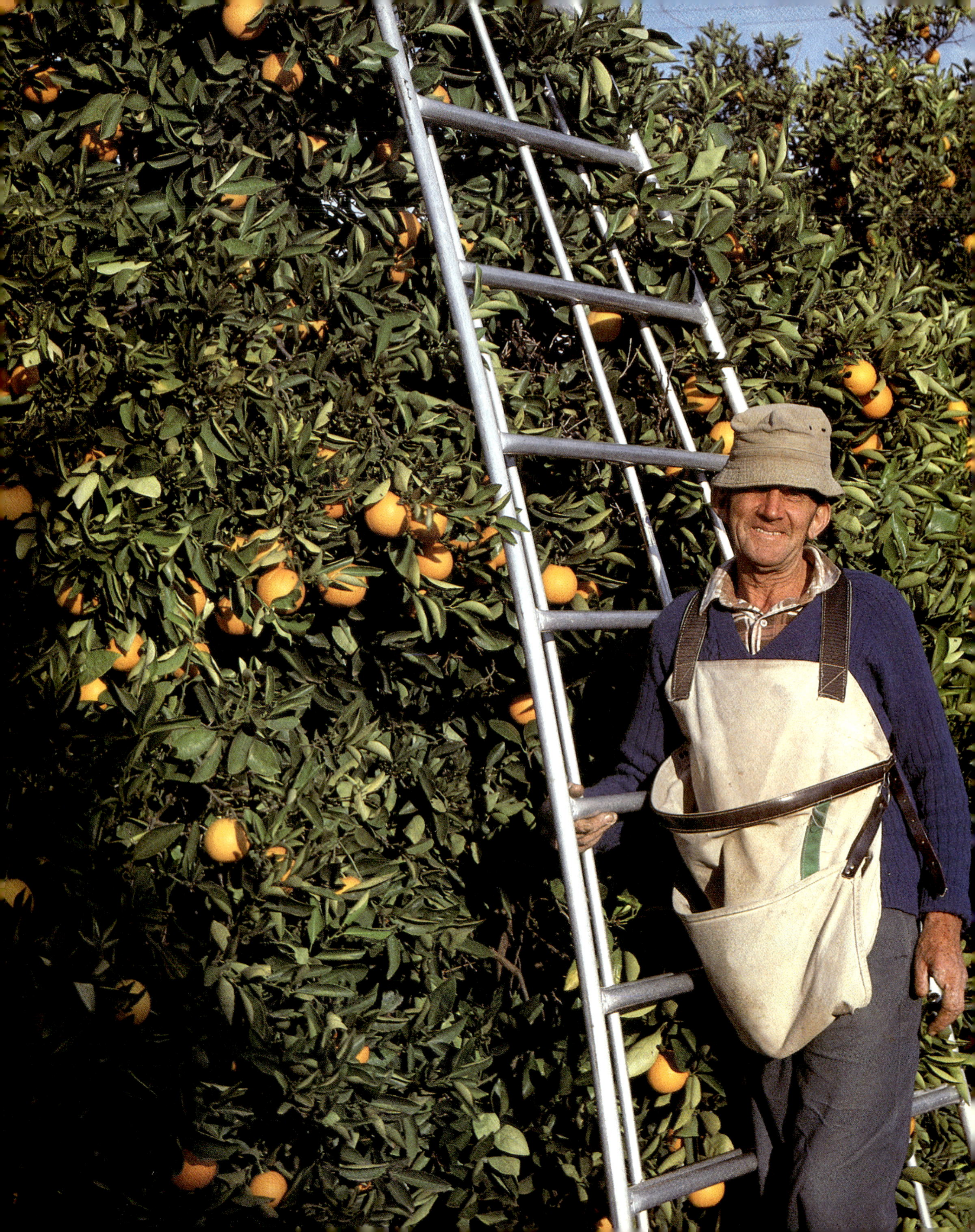

Orange pickers in South Australia's Riverland place the oranges they pick into the bag worn around the body. When this is unclipped from under the shoulders, the oranges roll out into a larger bin. The fruit then goes to the cannery at Berri or is transported to the markets.

Cutting and picking tobacco is one of the dirtiest jobs imaginable because of a brown sap that weeps from the leaves. Once dried, the tobacco is much more manageable.

Many southern European migrants who came to South Australia after World War II found work in vineyards. In the McLaren Vale area many of the grape pickers are Italian.

THE WORKERS 137

More recent migrants, from Vietnam, have also headed for McLaren Vale. Teams of labourers use secateurs to pick the grapes which are then dropped into little baskets. These in turn are tippped into a giant bin pulled along by a tractor and hauled off to the winery for crushing. Workers get paid by the basket.

For tomato pickers near Shepparton, Victoria the long day passes a little more quickly with the distraction of a radio.

THE WORKERS 139

Many of the Goulburn Valley pear pickers are women, who sometimes bring their children to work.

It was in a potato field in Dorrigo that Oliver found a worker he had imagined should exist, someone who has been in the world since Biblical times, who lives the verses: 'To everything there is a season, and a time to every purpose under the heaven; a time to be born, and a time to die; a time to plant, and a time to pluck up that which is planted'.

She was a strong, healthy-looking middle-aged woman who had been up since sunrise and out picking potatoes as white as full moons, in a field where the mist was still heavy and lying close to the ground. Her husband was working on a row nearby and two of her children, teenagers, were picking next to her. Oliver asked about her family. 'All my children grew up in a potato patch,' she laughed, 'except the youngest, who grew up in an onion patch.' As the day wore on her harvest became heavier – more like small lumps of lead nestling in the ground than freshly dug potatoes – and her stooped back, harder and harder to straighten.

Without doubt, it is easier to acquire gentlemanly deportment than axe-man's muscle; easier to recognise the various costly vintages than to live contentedly on the smell of an oily rag.
– *Such Is Life* by Joseph Furphy.

At 5.30 am, as the mist rolls over the paddocks, near Dorrigo in New South Wales, the only sound you can hear is the gentle 'bonk, bonk, bonk' of potatoes being dropped into tin buckets. The potatoes have been mechanically dug up, so that pickers can grade and collect them.

At the same time as pickers collect the potatoes they sort and size them. Only the most perfect potatoes are selected – they must be about the size of a clenched fist. Rejects are left behind on the ground.